The
Mystery
of Mysteries

Decoding the Divine Proportions of the Human Body Through
Art, Science, Anatomy, and Sacred Geometry

DAMIANO B. CENTOLA

EXPLORA BOOKS
700 – 838 West Hastings St. Vancouver, BC V6C 0A6
www.explorabooks.com
Phone: (604) 330 6795

Because of the dynamic nature of the Internet, any web addresses or links contained in this book may have changed since publication and may no longer be valid. The views expressed in this work are solely those of the author and do not necessarily reflect the views of the publisher, and the publisher hereby disclaims any responsibility for them.

Bible verses are quoted from the King James Version (KJV), which is public domain, the English Standard Version (ESV), and the New King James Version (NKJV).

ISBN: 978-1-997587-70-5 *(Paperback)*
978-1-83430-022-1 *(Hardback)*
978-1-83430-023-8 *(eBook)*

The
Mystery
of Mysteries

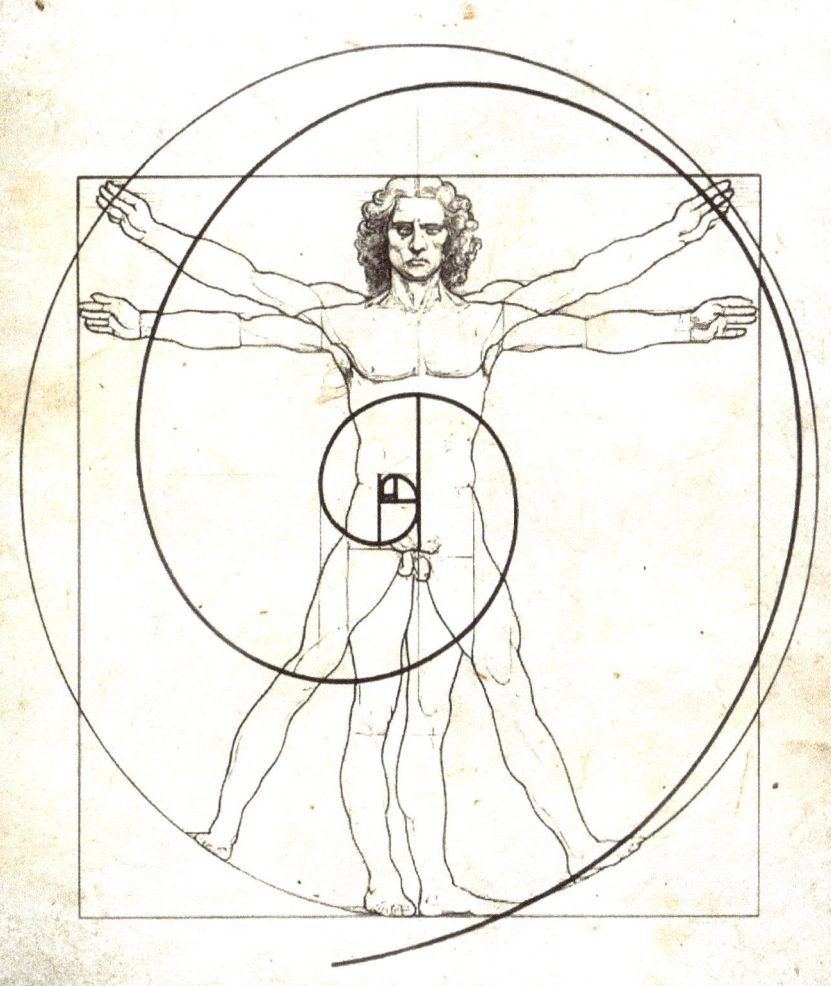

To Feebe Huang, whose love has been a true compass of grace.

To my father, Pop, and to my family members, whose lives have been living scrolls of devotion.

To my pastors and friends, who encouraged and walked beside me on this journey. And above all, to the Alpha and the Omega— the Aleph and the Tav, in whom circle and square are reconciled, and in whom all mysteries find their measure.

Table of Contents

Preface

Every book begins with a question. For me, the question was simple yet inexhaustible: Why did Leonardo da Vinci draw a man inside a circle and a square? That drawing—the Vitruvian Man—has been reproduced more than any other sketch in history. It hangs on classroom walls, adorns textbooks, and is hailed as the emblem of Renaissance genius. Yet behind its symmetry and proportion, I sensed something deeper: a hidden code, a sacred geometry not merely of art, but of creation itself.

This book was not born in an art studio or a lecture hall. It was born in prayer, in study, and in wonder at the Word of God. As I traced the lines of Leonardo's figure, I discovered that they echoed the lines of Scripture, the dimensions of the Tabernacle, the proportions of the Temple, and the mystery of Christ Himself. The journey that follows is not only mine—it belongs to anyone who has ever felt that the body is more than biology, that mathematics is more than numbers, and that art is more than beauty. It is the journey of rediscovering man as message: framed in square and circle, inscribed by breath and bone, measured by heaven and earth. I offer this work with humility and reverence, not as the final word on the subject, but as a testimony to the fact that the "mystery of mysteries" is written in us. The proportions of the human body, the geometry of the soul, and the eternal patterns of Scripture converge in a revelation that Leonardo hinted at, and that the Spirit confirms: we are fearfully and wonderfully made. My prayer is that as you read, you will not only see Da Vinci's drawing differently—you will see yourself differently. Not as random, but as radiant. Not as accidental, but as intentional. Not as silent, but as a living scroll of the Divine.

—Damiano B. Centola

Introduction

The Vitruvian Man is one of the most recognized drawings in the world. At first glance, it appears to be a simple study of proportion: a man, arms outstretched, inscribed within a square and a circle. For centuries, it has been explained as Leonardo da Vinci's visual commentary on Vitruvius, the Roman architect who taught that the human body contained the ideal measurements for temples and sacred structures. And yet, the drawing is more than geometry. It is a mystery. Why two poses, two sets of limbs? Why the square and the circle? Why the navel at the center of the circle, and the groin at the center of the square? Why did Leonardo write his notes in mirror script, as if concealing a secret? The answers are not exhausted by anatomy alone. They touch upon cosmology, mathematics, theology, and the eternal design of God. This book begins with the conviction that the Vitruvian Man is not merely an artistic exercise but a prophetic testimony. Leonardo did not simply capture symmetry; he unveiled something sacred. The drawing reveals man as both temple and messenger, both compass and scroll, both earthly and eternal. The journey ahead unfolds in three parts: 1. Foundations of Divine Design — where we explore the circle and the square, the dual poses, and the geometry that frames the body as both temporal and transcendent. 2. Anatomy of the Sacred — where the organs, bones, and breath themselves reveal divine meaning, echoing Scripture and temple design. 3. The Beyond — where the geometry of resurrection and the fulfillment of proportion in Christ declare that the human frame is not only created—it is redeemed. Along the way, we will trace the Golden Ratio in the body, the Fibonacci spiral in DNA, the resonance of organs, and the cruciform posture written into every human frame. But always, mathematics and anatomy will serve theology. For at the heart of this inquiry lies not da Vinci, nor Vitruvius, nor even geometry itself, but the truth of Scripture: that the body is the temple of the Holy Spirit, and that God has inscribed His wisdom into flesh and form. The reader should not expect a detached study of art history, nor a purely scientific analysis of anatomy. What follows is an integration of disciplines—art, mathematics, physiology, theology—woven into one tapestry. Like the drawing itself, it is both precise and poetic, both measurable and mysterious. In the end, the Vitruvian Man does not merely describe the human body. He describes us: who we are, why we exist, and how our very proportions testify to the One who framed us. This is the invitation of the mystery: to stand inside the square and the circle, to behold the cruciform posture of man, and to hear the eternal whisper inscribed in every line—"You are fearfully and wonderfully made."

— Damiano B. Centola

STEP ONE:

THE CIRCLE AND THE SQUARE— DUAL REALMS OF HUMAN EXISTENCE

"To measure a man by square and circle is to see his soul suspended between time and eternity."

DAMIANO B. CENTOLA

Chapter I
The Frame of the Divine

*"Before the temple was built in stone, it was formed
in flesh."*
— *Writer Damiano B. Centola*

The Forgotten Blueprint

In 1490, Leonardo da Vinci drew a man who would live forever.

Arms outstretched. Limbs extended. Two poses—one figure—contained within two perfect shapes: a square and a circle.

Above the image, Leonardo wrote in mirror-script: Le proporzioni del corpo umano secondo Vitruvio — The proportions of the human body according to Vitruvius.

But Leonardo did not merely sketch what he saw. He sketched what he understood—that man was not just anatomy, but a mystery. Not merely a body, but a design. Not just part of creation, but the very measure of creation itself.

What if the square and circle weren't just about balance and symmetry? What if they were the ancient language of the cosmos— reawakened in flesh?

To understand the true meaning of the Vitruvian Man, we must go to the root:

Why did Leonardo choose these shapes?

Why this pose?

Why this man?

What sacred knowledge was Da Vinci whispering through angles, ratios, and lines?

This chapter opens the first scroll.

The Language of Shapes: Earth and Eternity Long before numbers had symbols, they had shapes.

Sacred geometry spoke a silent language of Heaven and Earth. And within that language:

The square symbolized the earthly realm— structure, season, direction, dominion.

The circle represented the eternal realm—infinity, divinity, the spirit.

The square is built. The circle is born. The square is limited. The circle is limitless.

When Leonardo placed man within both, he wasn't just sketching proportional harmony. He was revealing a cosmic tension—man suspended between the temporal and the eternal.

The square grounds us. The circle surrounds us. And man—drawn inside—is the bridge.

Sacred Architecture and the Shape of God.

> *"He who measured the heavens first measured himself."*
> *—Writer Damiano B. Centola*

Da Vinci's inspiration, Vitruvius, was not just an architect—he was a philosopher of space. He believed the temple of man and the temple of God were not two separate structures. They echoed one another.

And so they do:

- In Exodus 27:1, the altar of sacrifice is built as a square.
- In 1 Kings 6:20, the Holy of Holies is a perfect cube—15x15x15 feet.
- In Revelation 21:16, the New Jerusalem is described as a city-square descending from Heaven, its length, width, and height equal.
- The sacred square governed the holiest spaces in history. Leonardo, knowing this, placed man inside the square—not to contain him, but to crown him as temple.
- First, temples were designed to reflect Heaven. Then, man was revealed as the original blueprint.

A Trinity in Lines: Vertical, Horizontal, Circular

Leonardo embedded a trinitarian structure into the drawing:

A vertical axis – connecting earth to heaven, symbolizing divine order.

A horizontal reach – the arms extended in a cross, representing time, space, and offering.

A fusion of circle and square – enclosing man in both the earthly and the eternal.

Man is not just in the frame.

Man is the frame.

The Gospel whispers beneath the lines:

> *"Your kingdom come, Your will be done, on earth as it is*
> *in heaven."*
> *—Matthew 6:10*

This prayer is not only verbal—it is architectural.

Centered by Design: Navel and Groin

Leonardo's geometry is exact. When man stands with arms extended and legs spread:

His navel aligns with the center of the circle. His groin aligns with the center of the square.

The navel—remnant of the womb—is the first connection to life, nourishment, and breath.

The groin—source of seed—is the place of legacy, fruitfulness, and dominion.

These dual centers preach a message:

You were born from above yet built to govern below.

You are both breath and bone, origin and offspring.

In theological terms:

Spirit and matter.

Heaven and earth.

Incarnation.

Phi, Pi, and the Divine Mathematics of Flesh

Modern anatomy confirms what Leonardo intuited: The golden ratio (1.618) appears in:

The head-to-body ratio.

The hand-to-forearm length.

The distance from the navel to the floor vs. the head to the navel.

The spiral of the ear, the structure of DNA, and even facial symmetry follow Fibonacci numbers.

Mathematics did not create the body. The body revealed the math.

And in this, we see:

God did not just create man beautifully—He created him intelligently.

We are not randomly assembled.

We are divinely engineered.

The Body as Compass and Cross.

The Vitruvian Man is also a directional map.

Arms reaching east and west.

Feet grounded north and south.

The body forming a perfect cruciform—a living compass.

In Hebrew, the word for "spirit" is ruach—wind, breath, direction.

In this design, man is not only the measured—he is the measurer. A temple with orientation.

You are the needle between what was and what will be. Your design points to the Divine.

The Body as Scroll: The Flesh Reads

In Jewish tradition, scrolls are unrolled, not opened. They are read line by line, slowly and reverently.

What if your body is a scroll?

The spine as the center axis—like a Torah scroll's wooden handles.

The bones as letters—rigid, structured, ancient.

The blood as ink.

The skin as parchment.

You are not just created—you are written.

And what's more: the message isn't simply to be read. It is to be revealed through motion, breath, and being.

Harmonics and the Sound of Design

The body is not silent.

The heart emits measurable electromagnetic waves.

The brain's alpha rhythms and DNA frequency emissions match the Earth's own resonance (7.83 Hz—Schumann Resonance).

The human voice creates resonant geometries in water, sand, and light.

Sound is not noise—it is shape.

The Word became flesh—and the flesh still echoes the Word.

Cruciform Revelation: The Pose of Sacrifice

Zoom out.

What shape does man take in the outer circle? A cross.

The square holds the flesh. The circle frames eternity. And man—stretched between—is a living crucifixion.

Leonardo never annotated this, but it's there:

Outstretched arms.

Head lifted.

Legs extended in dual pose—still and stepping. Man is not only the temple. Man is also the offering.

The Rediscovery of Sacred Science

Science today rediscovers what Leonardo and scripture already proclaimed:

> Fascia maps through the body like a geometric net—creating tension lines that resemble Vitruvian framing.
>
> The pineal gland sits perfectly centered between both hemispheres— often called the "seat of the soul."
>
> Sacred numbers like 3, 7, and 12 are embedded in the structure of ribs, vertebrae, and cranial bones.

The human body is not just a product of biology. It is the manifestation of divine information.

Final Reflection: The Frame is the Message

You are framed not to be contained—but to be revealed.

The square is the world.

The circle is the heavens.

And you—the Vitruvian man or woman—are the temple in between.

You are cruciform.

You are calculated.

You are cosmic.

You are called.

This is not a drawing.

This is a message.

This is you.

THE VITRUVIAN BODY

ANATOMICAL MEASUREMENTS FROM THE NAVEL

1 CORINTHIANS 6:19

THERE'S NO DEBATE - HERE ARE THE FACTS

The measurements speak...
The ratios align.

The head sits at 0,618 from
the navel-that's the golden
ratio, universaly
acknowledged in rature,

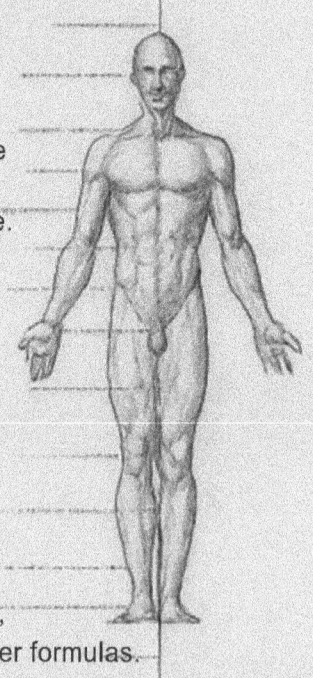

The organs fall into
symmetricamente-above
and below the navel-
like a divine architecture.
hidden in plain sight.

This isn't superstition.
This is structure.

This isn't a metaphor

This is math.
The human body is not
just biological-it's
theological. geometrical;
I'm not here to argue over formulas.

I'm here to unveil what's already
been carved into our frame by
the very breath of God.
"Do you not know that your body is
a temple of the Holy Spirit?"
This chart is the blueprint.

Damiano B. Centola

Chapter II

The Center of All Things

"To find the center of the universe, you must first locate the center of yourself."
—Writer Damiano B. Centola

What Lies at the Center

Leonardo da Vinci's Vitruvian Man is measured with such precision that everything begins from a single point: the center of the body. Not the brain.

Not the heart. But the navel—the quiet remnant of life's beginning.

Here, in the exact center of the circle enclosing the figure, is the place where all measurement begins.

But why the navel? Why not the heart or the head?

Because Leonardo knew what ancient sages, midwives, and mystics knew life begins with connection, not cognition.

The navel is our first link.

Where we were tethered, nourished, and grown.

It is the umbilical knot between origin and becoming.

It is both scar and seal, where dependence met design.

Vitruvian Body: Measurements from the Divine Center

Head (0.618 from center)

Eyes (0.493 from center)

Nose (0.448 from center)

Mouth/Jaw (0.398 from center)

Neck (0.368 from center)

Shoulders (0.318 from center)

Lungs (0.218 from center)

Heart (0.198 from center)

Diaphragm (0.168 from center)

Liver (0.118 from center)

Stomach (0.098 from center)

Kidneys (0.068 from center)

Da Vinci Center (Navel) Navel (0.0 from center)

Intestines (0.032 from center)

Pelvis (0.082 from center)

Reproductive Organs (0.132 from center)

Legs (0.182 from center)

Knees (0.282 from center)

Feet (0.382 from center)

The Navel as Origin Point: Scientific Insight

Modern embryology confirms what da Vinci drew.

- In utero, the navel is the central node from which the body radiates outward.
- All major organs form in symmetry around this point during early gestation.
- The vascular system emerges from the umbilical connection and grows out in divine spirals.

This means the human body is geometrically and biologically built outward from the navel— a living echo of the Big Bang within the womb.

You were not assembled.

You were spiraled into being.

Center and Sacred Space: The Tabernacle Parallel

In the Tabernacle, the center was always sacred.

- The Ark of the Covenant sat at the center of the Holy of Holies.
- The veil divided access to the center until it was torn.

Every piece of the Tabernacle was laid out in measured sequence around the center. In the same way:

- Your spine aligns vertically like a pillar.
- Your ribs arc around the center like temple walls.
- Your heart, just left of the center, pulses like an altar.

The center of your body is not empty. It is inhabited by purpose.

Divine Circles and the Womb of the World

Look again at the circle in Leonardo's drawing:

- It is drawn around the body, not above it.
- The navel is its center—suggesting not the crown of the head, but the source of life as the measuring line.

In sacred geometry, the circle is:

- A symbol of eternity
- A vessel of protection
- A cosmic womb

The ancient Hebrews called the womb rachamim— related to mercy, tenderness, and the divine feminine. God's mercies are womb-like— circling, nurturing, encompassing.

So is the circle.

So is your beginning.

So is the Vitruvian frame.

The Groin and the Square: The Dual Center

Leonardo also placed the groin at the center of the square. This is not just anatomical accuracy. It is symbolic design:

- The groin is where generational life is passed on.
- It represents authority, legacy, multiplication.

Together with the navel, it forms a dual revelation:

- The circle centers origin.
- The square centers dominion. You are both:
- Created by mercy
- Commissioned for mission

The Mathematical Heart of the Drawing

Leonardo's use of the center goes far beyond symbolism.

His entire figure is a study in radial geometry.

From the navel, he measures:

- The arc of the arms
- The length of the legs
- The tilt of the pelvis
- The curve of the ribs

This radial mapping mirrors what physicists now call radial symmetry— found in starfish, galaxies, and cellular division.

The body is not symmetrical by accident.

It is radial by design—as if everything you are expands outward from a divine epicenter.

The Temple Pattern in the Body

From the center, the human body maps onto the Temple of God:

Temple Element	Human Parallel
Outer Court	Skin & limbs
Inner Court	Organs
Holy of Holies	Navel / Heart

The Ark of the Covenant held three things:

1. The law (tablets) — Word
2. Manna — Bread
3. Aaron's staff — Authority

In the human body, the same realities appear in the living form:

1. DNA — the law of life
2. Blood — the life-source
3. Voice / Breath — the rod of command expressed through speech.

The temple was not just a house, it was a prophetic body.

And the body, in turn, is a living temple.

Psychological Centering: The Soul's Gravity

Psychologists speak of the need to be "centered."

But centering is not just emotional balance—it is a return to original alignment. Anxiety, depression, fear— all come from dislocation from our spiritual center.

- Centering prayer.
- Meditation on breath.
- Realigning the spine and breath with divine rhythm.

To be centered is to remember where you were first connected.

The Navel as the Throne of Stillness

Da Vinci did not center the body around motion.

He centered it in stillness.

The navel is:

- Quiet.
- Hidden.
- No longer active.

But it once gave everything, So too does God—often silent, often unseen—yet He is the source of every rhythm in your body and soul.

The center is not loud.

But from it comes life, design, order, identity.

Conclusion: The Center Is Calling

You were not made in chaos

You were measured from a center.

Your arms, your legs, your voice, your breath—all traceable back to that single point.

And that center still speaks. It says:

- You are not random.
- You are not forgotten.
- You are not empty.

You are measured.

You are framed.

You are known.

The center of the circle is not geometry.

It is glory. And it is calling you home.

The Cosmic Center and the Law of Correspondence

"As above, so below; as within, so without."

—Hermetic Axiom

From antiquity, sacred thinkers believed that the microcosm (man) reflected the macrocosm (the universe). The body was a universe in miniature—a cosmos with breath.

Leonardo's Vitruvian Man centers the body at the navel, just as many ancient cultures centered the universe around sacred mountains, trees, or temples:

> The Hebrews built the Temple on Mount Zion— believed to be the navel of the Earth (Ezekiel 38:12).

The Greeks placed the Omphalos stone at Delphi—the "center of the world," marked by Apollo.

In Buddhist cosmology, Mount Meru is the central pillar of existence— rising from the naval-point of the cosmic body.

These weren't metaphors. These were spatial declarations of meaning. The center of the world wasn't defined by geography. It was defined by divine connection.

And so, in your body:

> Your center is not your brain. It is not your ambition. It is your origin. Your umbilical truth.

The Geometry of Gestation: Spiraling from the Navel

Modern embryology shows that the first system to form in the womb is the vascular system—and it begins its formation from the umbilicus. Around it, the entire body forms in a spiraling, symmetrical pattern:

- The neural tube (precursor to the spinal cord) curves backward and upward.
- The limbs sprout outward from the central trunk like branches.
- The facial features develop in a radial pattern, folding toward symmetry.

Even more stunning: when visualized under high- definition scans, the blood vessels and nervous pathways around the umbilicus resemble sunbursts— like sacred mandalas.

The body is not just built from the center. It is bloomed.

Breath and Center: The Rhythm of Life

Your breathing is centered at the diaphragm, located above the navel. This sacred muscle:

- Divides upper and lower organs.
- Contracts rhythmically to allow the lungs to expand.
- Is shaped like a dome—a mini temple within the body.

In Hebrew, the word neshama (הָמָשְׁנ) means both breath and soul. Genesis 2:7 says:

> *"Then the Lord God formed man from the dust of the ground and breathed into his nostrils the breath of life…"*

That breath doesn't remain in the lungs. It travels— through the diaphragm, through the blood, and through every cell.

The center of your body is where spirit meets matter, where air becomes life, where breath becomes being.

And it moves in a divine rhythm:

- Inhale — Receive
- Exhale — Release

Christ and the Pierced Center

When Christ was crucified, He was pierced in the side— near the ribs, near the heart, near the center.

> *"One of the soldiers pierced His side with a spear, and immediately blood and water came out."*
> —John 19:34

This piercing at the center of His body became the birthplace of the Church—blood for atonement, water for baptism.

So it is with the body:

- From the center flows the covenant.
- From the center comes spiritual birth.

The navel is where life entered the womb.

The pierced side is where eternal life entered the world.

The Human Axis Mundi: You Are the Tree

In sacred cosmologies, the axis mundi (world axis) connects Heaven and Earth—often portrayed as:

- A tree (Tree of Life)
- A mountain (Sinai, Zion, Meru)
- A pillar (Jacob's ladder)

But what if that vertical axis lives in you?

- Your spine is the central tree.
- Your ribs are branches.
- Your center—the navel—is the root. In this design:
- Your head reaches Heaven.
- Your feet stand on Earth.
- And your center receives from both.
- You are the temple.
- You are the pillar.

You are the tree planted at the center of Eden.

Mapping the Universe Unto the Body

Modern physicists recognize that the universe may be radially expanding.

Just like the human body from the navel.

STEP TWO:
ARMS EXTENDED

'With arms outstreched, man does not reach for power—he reaches for Presence.'

DAMIANO B. CENTOLA

Da Vinci's decision to map the circle from the navel is prophetic:

- The cosmic microwave background radiation radiates evenly in every direction—like a divine ripple.
- The expanding galaxies echo the outward flow of life from a single center.
- The black hole's event horizon forms a perfect circle—mirroring the womb.

In other words:

The universe is not unlike you.

And you are not unlike the universe.

Conclusion: Return to the Center

The world will try to pull you in all directions—upward, outward, forward.

But wisdom begins not in movement, but in return.

Return to your breath. Return to your first tether.

Return to the place where you were known, shaped, and sent. The center of the circle is not a dot. It is a door.

Through it, all things begin. And to it, all things will return.

THE MYSTERY OF MYSTERIES—
STEP THREE
The Two Poses,
The Two Selves

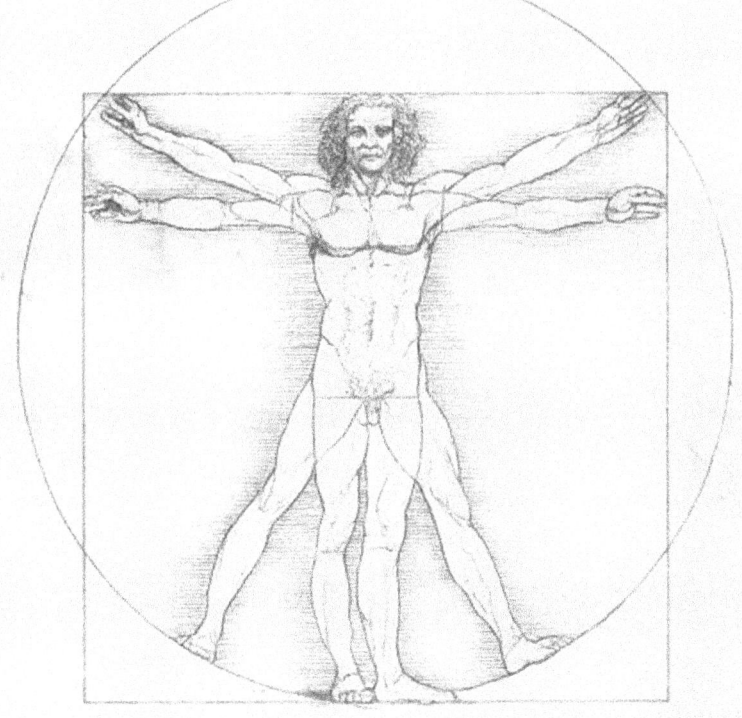

You were made in stillness to move.
Born into matter to rise in spirit—
Not just to occupy space—
But to stretch toward the Infinite.

Damiano B. Centola

Chapter III

The Two Poses, The Two Selves

"You were made to be still—and yet to reach. You are both fixed and in flight."

—*Writer Damiano B. Centola*

The Double Image: Stillness Meets Motion

When first encountering the Vitruvian Man, one might assume it is simply a man with limbs extended. But upon closer inspection, a mystery emerges:

Leonardo did not draw one pose—he drew two:

- One set of arms extended straight out horizontally.
- Another set raised at an angle.
- One set of legs held together.
- Another set stepping outward.

This was no artistic flourish. It was a coded revelation. Why draw two sets of limbs?

Why duplicate motion on a single frame? What is the soul of this superimposition?

Because Leonardo, in perfect symmetry and silence,

was declaring something bold:

You are two selves.

Two natures.

Two callings.

One design.

The Language of Duality in Creation

The world was created with a divine binary:

- Light and darkness
- Heaven and earth
- Male and female
- Spirit and flesh
- Stillness and motion

This is not division. This is design.

Genesis 1 reveals the rhythm of dual creation— "evening and morning," "waters above and waters below." This rhythm pulses in the cosmos and in the soul of man.

Leonardo's two poses reveal that man was made for balance:

- One pose is fixed—the earthly.
- One pose is reaching—the heavenly.

We are drawn between these two:

The self we are… and the self we are becoming.

The Inner Man and the Outer Man

Paul the Apostle writes in 2 Corinthians 4:16:

> *"Though our outer self is wasting away, our inner self is being renewed day by day."*

Leonardo drew them both:

- The outer man is physical, temporal, bound to gravity and aging.
- The inner man is eternal, spiritual, guided by truth and transformation.

The Vitruvian Man becomes a living parable:

- The lower set of limbs shows the anchored man—stable, finite, foundational.
- The upper set shows the ascending man— aspiring, open, transcendent.

Two poses.

One body.

One sacred contradiction.

The Physics of Superimposition

In quantum physics, particles exist in multiple states— superpositions—

until observed. They are neither one nor the other; they are both at once.

Leonardo's man is a superposition:

- He is still and in motion.
- At rest and in reach.
- Earthbound and heaven-struck.

This isn't confusion. It is revelation. You are not linear. You are layered.

Like light, which is both particle and wave—so you are:

- Matter and mystery
- Form and frequency
- Body and spirit

Stepping into Calling: The Pose of Movement

The legs in Vitruvian Man tell a story:

One pair stands firm.

The other pair steps outward—as if about to walk forward,

into purpose.

This is not random. It is a commission. Isaiah 30:21 says:

> *"Whether you turn to the right or to the left, your ears will hear a*
> *voice behind you saying,*
> *'This is the way; walk in it.'"*

Leonardo shows us that man is born in posture but destined for movement.

The stepping leg is the leg of faith—launching forward not because it sees the path, but because it was designed to move.

The Arms: Embrace and Surrender

Likewise, the arms stretch in two ways:

- One pair is horizontal—the arms of Christ, the arms of welcome, crucifixion, offering.
- The other pair is angled upward—the arms of worship, ascent, surrender.

This duality speaks of the heart of man:

- To offer and to receive
- To stretch out and to lift up
- To hold space and to reach Heaven.
- This is not contradiction.
- This is completion.

Biblical Echoes of Double Selves Scripture is full of dual identity:

- Jacob was Israel.
- Saul was Paul.
- Peter was Simon.

Christ was both Son of Man and Son of God.

Even the temple had two chambers—Holy Place and Most Holy Place.

Leonardo's dual-limbed man reflects this biblical pattern. He is the outer court and the inner fire—at once the vessel and the flame. Romans 7:22-23 speaks of this inner war:

> *"For in my inner being I delight in God's law, but I see another law at work..."*

The Vitruvian pose captures that tension—one self-fixed in frame, the other pulling forward into transformation.

The Two Selves in the Psalms and Prophets

King David often spoke to himself:

"Why are you cast down, O my soul?" (Psalm 42:5) "Bless the Lord, O

my soul."

(Psalm 103:1)

Why?

Because he knew he was more than one voice.

Leonardo's drawing echoes that sacred split: you are self and soul, mind and mystery, dust and divinity.

The Sacrament of Duality: Christ the Vitruvian

The crucifixion itself is the ultimate revelation of the Two Selves:

- Christ in the flesh—wounded, bleeding, hanging.
- Christ in the spirit—forgiving, redeeming, reigning.

Vitruvian Man, arms outstretched, limbs in motion, becomes an image of that very tension:

- The man fully given to earth.
- The man fully surrendered to Heaven.

He is both Adam… and the Second Adam. Both man… and God.

And so are you—in Christ, walking the frame of earth while bearing the imprint of eternity.

Conclusion: Be Both

You do not need to choose between:

- Stillness and motion
- Body and spirit
- Breath and fire

You were designed to hold the contradiction. You are a temple. You are a traveler.

You are stretched between Earth and Heaven.

Leonardo gave us two poses not to confuse us, but to remind us: We are not either/or. We are both/and.

You are not half of something.

You are the whole image of a God who came to dwell in tension—so that you could walk in truth.

The Geometry of Becoming: Leonardo's Grids and Hidden Lines

Leonardo da Vinci's notebooks reveal his obsession with grids—not just for anatomy, but for transformation.

Behind the Vitruvian Man lies an implied structure of lines and proportions:

- The vertical axis divides the body into left and right—symbolizing duality.
- The horizontal axis marks balance and outreach—arms extended, a cruciform.
- But the two poses imply movement through space and time, like the beginning and end of a sacred dance.

This is the geometry of becoming. The grid is not just a frame. It's a portal between versions of the self:

- The man you were
- The man you are
- The man you are becoming Da Vinci did not only draw a body.

He drew a timeline, intersecting itself in holy pause.

The Doctrine of the Two Adams

The Bible speaks of two men who represent the human race:

- The first Adam — formed from dust, brought sin and death.
- The second Adam, Christ — came from Heaven, brought life and redemption.

Paul writes in 1 Corinthians 15:45:

> *"The first man Adam became a living being; the last Adam became a life- giving spirit."*

Leonardo's double-pose can be seen as:

- The first Adam—legs together, grounded in the square.
- The second Adam—arms raised, stepping outward, reaching the circle.

Vitruvian Man becomes a visual gospel:

- Two forms
- Two covenants
- One fulfilled design

Psychological Duality: The Shadow and the Light

Carl Jung wrote that every human has a shadow self— the unexpressed or repressed version of who we are. In his studies on alchemy, symbols, and the self, Jung pointed to the image of the mandala—a circle that represents the integration of opposites.

Da Vinci's circle is not just a geometric enclosure. It is a mandala of the soul.

Inside it, you are:

- Saint and sinner
- Finite and infinite
- Known and unknown The two poses suggest:
- A self that is safe and centered
- And a self that is reaching and vulnerable

Healing comes not by choosing one—but by embracing both.

You are not divided to be destroyed.

You are doubled to be discovered.

Motion in the Still Frame: Divine Kinetics

Though the Vitruvian Man is still, his limbs in motion create implied movement. Artists call this contrapposto— a pose suggesting energy and transition.

In Scripture, moments of stillness and motion are often paired:

> *"Be still and know that I am God." (Psalm 46:10) "Go, therefore, into all nations..."*
> *(Matthew 28:19)*

Stillness brings awareness.

Motion brings mission.

Leonardo encoded this tension:

- The man stands, but moves.
- The man rests, but ascends.
- You were not drawn to stay still.

You were measured to move with revelation.

Ancient Symbols of Duality: From Egypt to Eden

Throughout ancient cultures, divine figures were often portrayed in mirrored poses:

- The Egyptian god Horus often appeared with one hand down, one hand up—symbolizing life and death.
- In Hindu iconography, Shiva's Nataraja pose contains arms in four different directions—creating balance between destruction and creation.
- The Tree of Life in Genesis was placed in the middle of the garden—between knowledge of good and evil.

Leonardo's Vitruvian Man follows the same eternal pattern:

- Two arms – one that gives, one that receives
- Two legs – one that stands, one that walks
- One body – suspended in divine symmetry

Balance is not the absence of tension. Balance is divine integration.

The Crossroads of the Soul: Where Selves Meet

Every person will stand at the place where these two selves meet:
The self that fears change and wants to stay in the square.
The self that hungers for purpose and reaches for the circle.
Jesus met this crossroads in Gethsemane:

"Not my will, but Yours be done."

That moment was a duality resolved.
So too must each of us choose—daily:

- To remain… or to reach.
- To guard… or to grow.
- To fear… or to follow.

The two poses are not just anatomy. They are decision points—etched in bone.

The Glory of Dual Image: You Are Meant to Hold Both

The glory of Vitruvian Man is that he contains both.

- Both poses.
- Both expressions.
- Both natures. You were made to:
- Stand grounded in who you are…
- While stepping forward into who you're becoming.

You are the intersection of:

- Faith and logic
- Heaven and earth
- Dust and divinity

This is not spiritual schizophrenia. This is sacred synergy. God made you as a paradox to reveal His perfection.

Final Revelation: You Are the Bridge

In the end, the Vitruvian Man is not a contradiction. He is a bridge.

- Between the two poses
- Between the two selves
- Between the two realms You were made to:

- Stretch wide
- Step forward
- Live in tension
- And be whole in it all

This is the final truth of the double image: You are not split. You are sanctified in symmetry.

You are one man, two frames, one eternal purpose.

STEP FOUR: THE NAVEL AND THE GROIN – THE TWIN CENTERS OF CREATION

The navel remembers
where life began;
the groin declares
where life begins again.

Damiano B. Centola

Chapter IV

The Horizontal Revelation

"Stretch out your arms—not only to measure the world, but to offer yourself to it."

—Writer Damiano B. Centola

The Line That Divides and Connects

Leonardo da Vinci's Vitruvian Man is not merely a body drawn within shapes. He is a cross in motion.

- His arms, in one of the two poses, are stretched outward horizontally.
- His chest becomes the center.
- The body forms a perfect horizontal axis, dividing top and bottom, left and right.

But this horizontal line is not just anatomical. It is cosmic.

It is the line of offering. The line of incarnation. The line of the cross.

The Cruciform Revelation: A Living Cross

What shape do we see?

- Head lifted.
- Arms outstretched.
- Feet fixed and parted.

It is the shape of a living crucifixion.

This was no coincidence. Leonardo knew the symmetry of the human body was not just architectural, but theological. The Vitruvian Man mimics the exact geometry of Christ on the cross.

Philippians 2:7–8 says:

> *"He emptied himself, taking the form of a servant... and humbled himself by becoming obedient to the point of death— even death on a cross."*

The horizontal line is the gesture of surrender:

- Arms open.
- Nothing withheld.
- Fully revealed.

It is the posture of Christ.

And it is drawn into the geometry of every human being.

The Arms of Eden: Open or Closed

In Eden, Adam and Eve hid—covering themselves.

But in Leonardo's man, the arms are wide open, palms extended outward.

This is vulnerability.

This is invitation.

It says:

> *"Here I am—fully measured, fully known, unhidden."*

This is the posture of:

- Worship
- Surrender
- Covenant

It is also the posture of Adam restored—the man who no longer hides from God, but stretches wide to be seen, searched, and sanctified.

The Horizontal Axis in the Temple

The tabernacle was built on a grid—its layout divinely dictated.

- North and South: altars, courts, and gates.
- East and West: entrance and the Ark.
- Center: the place where priest meets God.

The Holy Place and Most Holy Place are divided by a horizontal veil,

separating man from the presence— until Christ tore it.

So too in the human body:

- The arms divide upper and lower.
- The ribs form an arch, a sanctuary of breath.
- The heart, behind the center of the arms, becomes the ark of the covenant.

The arms are not just limbs.

They are curtains, opening the sacred place within.

Anatomical Geometry: The Winged Measure

Leonardo's choice to extend the arms straight out transforms the man

into a T-shape.

- The wingspan of the arms equals the height of the body— approximately one-to-one.
- This is the human square, the measurable foundation of da Vinci's design.

But more than a square, it becomes a cross.

In Hebrew, the ancient letter Tav (ת) looked like a cross and symbolized:

- Truth
- Covenant
- Marking the redeemed

You were drawn with arms outstretched… because you were made to

bear the sign of truth and redemption.

The Posture of Embrace and Expansion

When you stretch your arms wide:

- You create space for others.
- You expose your vital organs—it's an act of trust.
- You become a bridge—linking what's on your left and right.

This posture:

- Embraces.
- Welcomes.
- Connects.

You are no longer closed, curled, or clenched. You are wide open.

The horizontal revelation is the truth that man was made to offer himself—fully, sacrificially, and gloriously.

The Cross as Sacred Geometry

The cross is not merely an instrument of death. It is:

- A vertical line (Heaven to Earth)
- A horizontal line (Man to Man) Jesus fulfilled both.

And the Vitruvian Man, arms stretched along that same horizontal line, mirrors the Gospel:

- The vertical reaches for God.
- The horizontal embraces the world. The result?

The body becomes a temple, a bridge, and a living offering—all in one posture.

Neuroscience of the Horizontal Line

Scientific studies now show that humans extend their arms outward, the brain:

- Activates regions associated with trust, invitation, and emotional openness.
- Reduces cortisol—our stress hormone.
- Increases oxytocin—our bonding hormone.

This means:

> Leonardo's posture is not just beautiful.

> It is biologically healing.

To open your arms is to open your brain.

To expand your chest is to relieve your burden. The posture of Vitruvian Man is a posture of peace.

The Horizontal Line in the Heavens

Even in the cosmos, horizontal lines matter:

- The horizon divides heaven from earth—where light meets land.
- The ecliptic plane of the solar system is horizontal—where planets orbit in balance.
- The galactic equator cuts across the Milky Way— a mirror of the body's symmetry.

As above, so within:

> The outstretched arms mirror the heavens—a celestial orientation

> embedded in your flesh.

The Body as Offering, Not Just Object

With arms stretched wide:

- You are not just seen.
- You are given. You become:
- An offering.
- A vessel.
- A blessing.

This is why Christ didn't resist the nails—because He knew that the

horizontal posture was the doorway to resurrection.

So, it is for us:

- You were not meant to fold inward.
- You were made to stretch, give, welcome, surrender.

Final Reflection: Let the Arms Preach

Your arms preach a gospel:

- Not of clenched fists, but open palms.
- Not of holding back, but opening wide.
- Not of domination, but of embrace.

The horizontal line is the line of invitation:

Come.

Be known.

Be measured.

Be redeemed.

You were not drawn for isolation.

You were measured to reach—both across and beyond.

Arms of the Ancient Gods: A Universal Symbol

In civilizations spanning millennia, outstretched arms conveyed power, prayer, and presence:

- Egyptian gods like Horus and Isis were often depicted with extended wings—symbolizing protection and divine embrace.
- In Babylonian reliefs, rulers stood with arms wide, invoking the favor of gods.

In Hindu iconography, arms extended in mudras (sacred gestures) expressed cosmic truths.

Even in Buddhist art, the standing Buddha's open arms symbolized openness to suffering and compassion.

Da Vinci captured this eternal posture of divinity—but placed it inside man.

The arms of Vitruvian Man are not about domination. They are about divine embodiment.

Leonardo tells us:

The pose of the gods is also the posture of man.

The Horizontal as Covenant

Throughout scripture, covenants are enacted with outstretched hands:

- Moses lifts his arms to keep Israel victorious (Exodus 17:11–12).
- Priests bless the people with upraised palms (Leviticus 9:22).
- Christ blesses the disciples before ascending— arms extended (Luke 24:50).

Even in suffering, the arms of God remain open:

> *"All day long I have held out my hands to a disobedient and*
> *contrary people."*
> —*Romans 10:21*

The horizontal axis is the axis of mercy.

God doesn't point with fingers—He opens arms.

Arms and the Power of Presence Psychology confirms the power of posture. People who:

- Keep arms closed are seen as defensive, self- protective.
- Extend arms are perceived as confident, trustworthy, magnetic.

This applies to public speaking, negotiation, and even worship. Vitruvian Man, frozen in time, proclaims:

> ➢ You were made for openness.
> ➢ Your spirit thrives when your body agrees with your truth.

To live with outstretched arms is to live unafraid of presence—yours and God's.

The Architecture of Outreach

Temples, cathedrals, and basilicas mirror the human form:

- The nave (center aisle) reflects the spine.
- The transepts (cross arms of the structure) stretch horizontally, like the arms of a cruciform body.
- The altar sits at the center—parallel to the heart.

Leonardo, having studied such structures, understood:

> The architecture of the church mirrors the posture of the man
> within the circle and square.

This means:
- You are not just the temple.
- You are the crossbeam within it.

Your arms—like transepts—extend outward to carry presence into the world.

Horizontal Line as Mission

Jesus said in John 12:32:

"And I, if I be lifted up from the earth, will draw all men unto me."

The lifting is vertical.

The drawing is horizontal. Every act of love stretches:
- Toward another.
- Toward the wounded.
- Toward the lost.

The Vitruvian arms speak:

"You are the reach of God."

"You are the bridge between soul and soil."

And like Christ, your arms are not just anatomical.

They are missional.

The Human Cross in Leonardo's Mind

In his notebooks, Leonardo references:

- The ratio of the arm span to the height as a divine proportion.
- The idea that man, with arms stretched wide, could be fitted into a square—the perfect container of matter.

But he didn't stop there. He added the circle, implying spirit, eternity, and transcendence.

TO ME, THERE'S NO DEBATE—HERE ARE THE FACTS.

THE MEASUREMENTS SPEAK. THE RATIOS ALIGN THE HEAD SITS AT 0.618 FROM THE NAVEL– THAT'S THE GOLDEN RATIO UNIVERSALLY ACKNOWLEDGED IN NATURE, ART, AND SACRED DESIGN, THE ORGANS FALL INTO SYMMETRICAL PLACEMENTS ABOVE AND BELOW THE NAVEL—LIKE A DIVINE ARCHITECTURE HIDDEN IN PLAIN SIGHT.

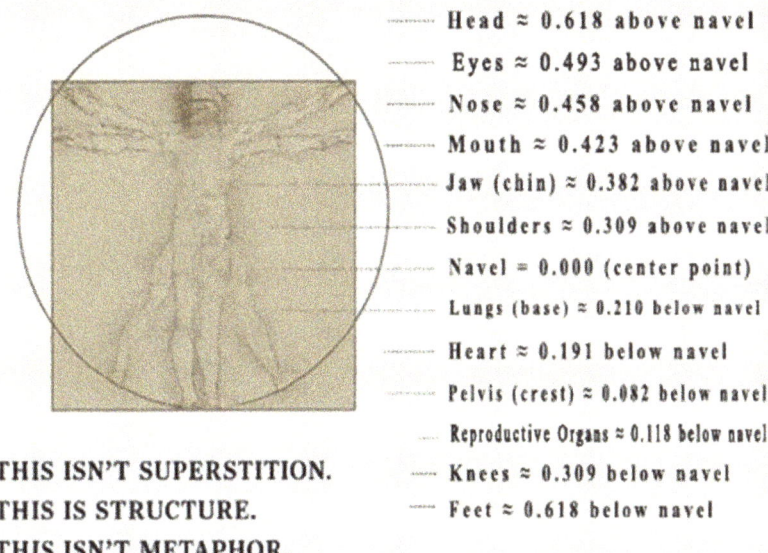

- Head ≈ 0.618 above navel
- Eyes ≈ 0.493 above navel
- Nose ≈ 0.458 above navel
- Mouth ≈ 0.423 above navel
- Jaw (chin) ≈ 0.382 above navel
- Shoulders ≈ 0.309 above navel
- Navel = 0.000 (center point)
- Lungs (base) ≈ 0.210 below navel
- Heart ≈ 0.191 below navel
- Pelvis (crest) ≈ 0.082 below navel
- Reproductive Organs ≈ 0.118 below navel
- Knees ≈ 0.309 below navel
- Feet ≈ 0.618 below navel

THIS ISN'T SUPERSTITION.
THIS IS STRUCTURE.
THIS ISN'T METAPHOR.
THIS IS MATH.

THE HUMAN BODY ISN'T JUST BIOLOGICAL– IT'S *THEOLOGICAL* GEOMETRICAL, AND INTENTIONAL.

I'M NOT HERE TO ARGUE OVER FORMULAS. I'M HERE TO UNVEIL WHAT'S ALREADY BEEN CARVED INTO OUR FRAME BY THE VERY BREATH OF GOD.'

Damiano B. Centola

The result:

> A man caught in earthly dimension (square) And heavenly circumference (circle).
>
> The horizontal arms become the hinge between these realms.
>
> The arms aren't where the drawing ends.
>
> They are where movement begins.

Final Reflection: You Were Drawn to Open

Leonardo could have drawn the man standing straight, arms at his sides.

But he didn't.

He chose to stretch the arms. To expose the chest.

To make man vulnerable and vast.

Why?

Because this is what God does. He opens.

He gives. He blesses.

And He formed man to do the same.

Your arms are not weapons. They are wings. They are altars.

They are the welcome of God in the world.

To stretch horizontally is to say:

> I am not hiding.
>
> I am not afraid.
>
> I am here to love.

Step Five

Ratios of God – Proportions, Mathematics, and Sacred Order

"Divine order does not guess—
it measures. Every line,
every limb, drawn
with eternal precision."

– Damiano B. Centola

Chapter V
Divine Symmetry and Sacred Math

"You are more than balanced—you are built by beauty, encoded in eternal proportion."
—Writer Damiano B. Centola

The Signature of the Divine

Leonardo da Vinci once wrote:

> *"There is no higher form of knowledge than that which reads the language of mathematics in the flesh of the world."*

But Leonardo did not just read that language—he wrote it into the Vitruvian Man.

At the heart of his design lies symmetry—but not the mechanical kind.

This is divine symmetry:

- A balance between order and wonder
- A harmony between function and form
- A beauty that is not just pleasing, but prophetic.

And behind it all is a number—the number 1.618… The Golden Ratio. Also known as phi (φ).

This is the fingerprint of God.

Not only seen in nature—but carved into you.

The Mystery of Mysteries

What Is the Golden Ratio?

The Golden Ratio is a mathematical constant:

- Approximately 1.6180339887…
- It appears when a line is divided into two parts, such that the whole length divided by the long part is equal to the long part divided by the short.

This number:

- Has no end.
- Has no pattern.
- Cannot be simplified.

It is irrational… yet divinely rational. It appears in:

- Spiral galaxies
- Seashells
- Sunflower seeds
- Hurricanes
- Human faces
- DNA helices
- The proportions of your hand, arm, and entire body.
- It is not a coincidence.

It is a constant whisper—embedded in creation.

The Golden Ratio in the Human Body

Leonardo da Vinci did not invent these proportions. He discovered them—and drew them.

The Vitruvian Man is built on phi:

- The ratio of your forearm to hand ≈ 1.618
- The height of your head to your torso ≈ 1.618
- The distance from shoulder to fingertip/elbow to fingertip ≈ 1.618
- The navel to head/navel to feet ≈ 1.618

Every major line Leonardo drew obeys this ratio— because your body is a golden instrument.

You are not just flesh. You are math in motion.

Fibonacci:

The Number Sequence of Life.

The Golden Ratio is closely linked to the Fibonacci sequence:

0, 1, 1, 2, 3, 5, 8, 13, 21, 34, 55, 89, 144…

Each number is the sum of the two before it.

And the further along the sequence you go, the closer the ratio between successive numbers approaches phi.

In the body:

- You have 2 eyes, 5 fingers, 8 bones in the wrist, 13 major joints in the hand and arm.
- Even the distance between heartbeats, when measured in micro- vibrations, pulses in Fibonacci-based waveforms.

The breath of God is structured.

It counts.

It curves.

It builds.

And it spirals into being.

Sacred Math in Sacred Texts

The Bible is filled with sacred numbers:

- 3 – Trinity, resurrection, completeness
- 7 – Divine order, Sabbath, perfection
- 12 – Tribes, disciples, foundation
- 40 – Testing, transformation
- 144 – Found in Revelation, linked to temple design ad Fibonacci sequence

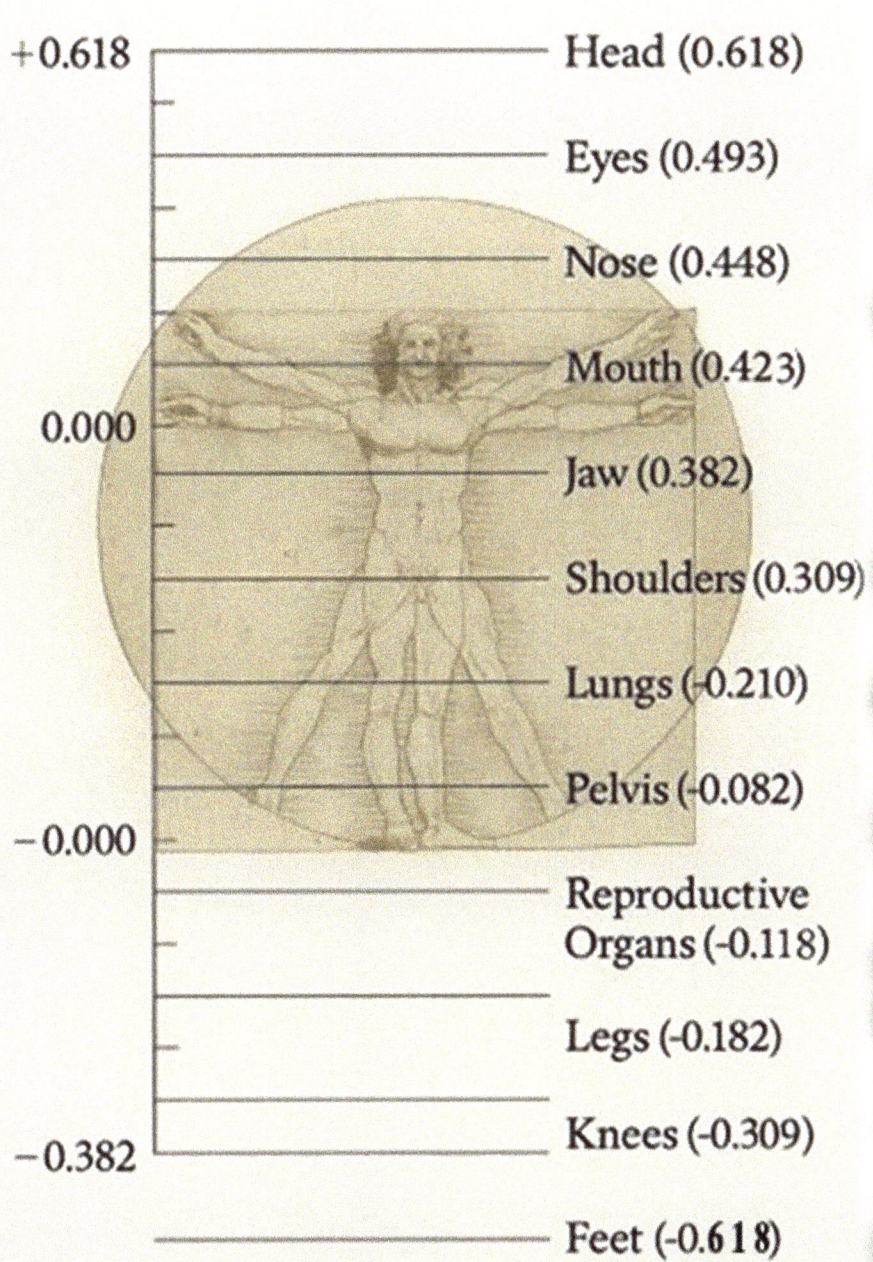

+0.618 — Head (0.618)

Eyes (0.493)

Nose (0.448)

Mouth (0.423)

0.000 — Jaw (0.382)

Shoulders (0.309)

Lungs (-0.210)

Pelvis (-0.082)

-0.000 — Reproductive
Organs (-0.118)

Legs (-0.182)

Knees (-0.309)

-0.382 —

Feet (-0.618)

In 1 Kings 6:20, Solomon's temple is described as 20 cubits by 20 cubits by 20 cubits—a perfect cube.

In Revelation 21:16, the New Jerusalem is described as 12,000 stadia in length, width, and height.

Leonardo's Vitruvian Man stands as a temple-body:

- Measured in numbers known to Scripture.
- Positioned in ratios foretold by design.
- You were not only made.

You were measured—by eternal mathematics.

Geometry and the Soul

Pythagoras taught that the soul is formed in proportion:

- Harmony of the soul = harmony of the body
- The triangle, square, and circle were seen as the shapes of the soul's formation

In Leonardo's drawing:

- The square reflects the world—the four corners, four winds, four elements.
- The circle reflects the eternal.
- The intersecting human body is the bridge.

His limbs form triangles, his stance suggests ratios, his reach defines arcs. You are not abstract.

You are defined by divine dimension.

Pi and the Circular Design

The circle in the Vitruvian Man is governed by π (pi $\approx$ 3.14159)—the ratio of a circle's circumference to its diameter.

Pi is infinite. Like phi, it never ends.

But while phi governs growth, pi governs completion:

- Circles
- Time
- Cycles
- Orbits

And it governs you:

- Your joints rotate in circular arcs
- Your vision sweeps in curved patterns
- Your muscles contract in curves

Da Vinci's use of both square and circle—pi and phi— declares: You are not only growth.

You are completion in progress.

DNA and Divine Ratio

Even your cellular code—DNA—obeys phi.

- The spiral staircase of DNA curves at exact phi angles
- The distance between each full twist of the double helix? 34 angstroms.
- The width of the helix? 21 angstroms.

34 and 21—two consecutive Fibonacci numbers. And $34 \div 21 \approx 1.619\ldots$

Your very blueprint obeys sacred math.

You are not merely biological.

You are numeric poetry encoded in flesh.

The Music of the Ratios

Musical harmony is mathematical.

- Octaves double (2:1)
- Perfect fifths (3:2)
- Major sixths (5:3)
- The entire musical scale follows Fibonacci spacing

Leonardo played the lyre and understood this.
He saw that the body resonates like an instrument:

- The rib cage like a soundboard
- The spine like a neck
- The lungs like bellows

You are not just formed. You are tuned.

When God breathed into Adam, He didn't just give life.

He gave resonance.

Final Reflection:

You Are the Equation

You are:

- Phi in posture
- Pi in breath
- Fibonacci in motion
- Geometry in soul

You are the:

- Temple
- Music
- Mathematics
- Mirror of the cosmos

You are not a mistake.

You are a mathematical miracle.

Divine symmetry made visible.

Leonardo revealed this by drawing a man.

But you—You reveal it by being one.

STEP SIX

THE NUMBER FOUR—
CROSS AND COMPASS

"Four is the number of foundation—earth, seasons, limbs, Gospels. It is not coincidence. It is code."

— DAMIANO B. CENTOLA

Chapter VI

The Eyes, the Ears, the Jaw—What the Organs Preach

"Every part of you is a parable. Every organ is a sermon in shape, sound, and sacrifice."
—Writer Damiano B. Centola

The Anatomy of Meaning

Leonardo da Vinci, in his anatomical drawings, went beyond the bone and muscle. He etched each organ with reverence, as if it held a hidden voice.

This chapter begins where most end: within the body.

We now measure from the inside out—not just to map the form, but to discover the message embedded in:

- The eyes, which perceive both light and soul.
- The ears, which receive frequency, not just sound.
- The jaw, which shapes the spoken word—the tool of creation.

You are not just made to function.

You were made to speak design through your organs.

The Eyes: The Geometry of Perception

Jesus said.

"The eye is the lamp of the body..."
—Matthew 6:22

The eye is a sphere—a circle, nested with circles:

- Iris
- Pupil
- Retina
- Cornea

Each layer is a sacred veil—filtering light to reveal vision. But the eye does more than see. It:

- Interprets reality
- Mirrors the soul
- Projects and receives emotion

Leonardo knew this.

His studies of optics show how light bends and fractures through the eye—how a straight beam is shaped into meaning.

Spiritually, the eye preaches:

- Discernment
- Light-bearing
- Intuition

Its spherical shape echoes the circle of the heavens.

You do not simply look.

You perceive prophecy.

The Ears: The Architecture of Frequency

The ear is shaped like a spiral. This spiral:

- Echoes the Fibonacci sequence.
- Amplifies vibration into understanding.
- Is formed in the womb before hearing begins— suggesting design precedes sound.

The cochlea, deep within the ear, contains fluid-filled chambers that convert movement into electrical signals for the brain. This is liquid-to-light translation.

And yet, what is hearing in scripture?

> *"Faith comes by hearing, and hearing by the word of God."*
> —*Romans 10:17*

The ear is faith's doorway.

Its geometry is not accidental:

- It curves inward.
- It spirals toward center.
- It draws revelation inward, where the soul decodes it.

The ears do not simply detect sound. They tune the soul to Heaven's voice.

The Jaw: The Instrument of Command

No part of the body is more weighted with spiritual authority than the jaw.

- It holds the tongue.
- It anchors the voice.
- It moves the mandate of man.

In Genesis, God spoke creation into existence. In Exodus, Moses spoke to Pharaoh.

In John, Christ is called the Word made flesh. And from your jaw:

- You speak truth or lies.
- You bless or curse.
- You echo God or mimic man.

Leonardo's anatomical sketches of the temporomandibular joint (TMJ) show it as a hinge—a pivot between silence and speech.

The jaw is not bone. It is a gate.

The Mouth: The Altar of Breath

Proverbs 18:21 says:

"Death and life are in the power of the tongue."

Behind the lips lies the mouth—arched like a temple ceiling, wrapped in muscle and nerve.

It is:

- The gateway of speech
- The channel of breath
- The doorway of praise

The palate (roof of the mouth) mirrors the vault of a cathedral.

When you sing or speak, resonance fills that space—like incense rising in the temple.

The mouth is not just biological. It is liturgical.

Bones that Whisper: What the Skull Tells Us

Leonardo studied the skull like a sculptor:

- It houses the brain (mind)
- Protects the eyes (sight)
- Anchors the ears (hearing)
- Frames the mouth (speech)

The shape of the cranium is almost spherical—once again, echoing the cosmic design.

In rabbinic tradition, the skull was called the Gulgoleth—the place of covering.

And yet… it is at Golgotha—the Place of the Skull—that Christ was crucified.

What does this preach?

That redemption happened at the seat of reason.

That divine glory shattered human limitation at the top of man.

The Organs and Their Sacred Frequencies

Modern science has discovered that the human body functions through layered rhythms:

The heart beats at roughly 1–1.5 Hz (Pulse Rhythm)

The breath cycles at approximately 0.2–0.4 Hz (Respiratory Rhythm).

The brain Waves:

- Delta: 0.5–4 Hz
- Theta: 4–8 Hz
- Alpha: 8–12 Hz
- Beta: 12–30 Hz

Leonardo did not have EEGs or ultrasound —but he observed what we now understand:

- The body pulses.
- The organs speak in rhythm.
- The human form is an orchestra.

Each organ is like an instrument in an orchestra:

- The lungs are the wind.
- The heart is percussion.
- The mouth is the horn.
- The brain is the conductor.

You are not only designed. You are composed.

The Temple Blueprint and the Organs Within

Just as the Tabernacle had three parts:

1. Outer Court (body)
2. Holy Place (soul)
3. Most Holy Place (spirit)

So, the body has three primary levels:

1. Senses and limbs (Outer Court)
2. Organs and emotions (Holy Place)
3. Breath, spirit, soul (Most Holy Place)

The organs, then, are not just tools.

They are the furnishings of the temple.

- The heart is the altar.
- The liver is the laver—cleansing, filtering.
- The lungs are the incense—breath offered.

The brain is the lampstand—illumination and memory.

When you breathe… you offer incense.

When your heart beats… the altar burns.

When you speak… the Word is carried forth.

Conclusion: Let the Body Preach

Leonardo studied the body to draw it.

You are called to study it to hear it.

- The eyes see truth.
- The ears receive God's voice.
- The jaw speaks identity.
- The skull holds divine consciousness.

The Vitruvian Man, when read from the inside, becomes a scroll of sacred anatomy.

Each part is poetry. Each shape is sermon. Each function is flame. Your body is not just designed. It is declaring.

The Lungs: The Incense of Breath

The lungs are the worship leaders of the body.

- Two chambers.
- Shaped like wings.
- Opening and closing in sacred rhythm.
- Each inhale is receiving.
- Each exhale is offering.

In Hebrew, the word for breath is ruach— the same word for spirit and wind. In Greek, pneuma. In Latin, spiritus. In Chinese, qi.

In all languages, the concept is the same:

Breath is not just survival—it is divine flow.

The alveoli—tiny air sacs within the lungs—number in the hundreds of millions, spreading like tree branches, delivering life to every corner.

The bronchial tree even resembles the Tree of Life in reverse—rooted in the mouth, branching deep into the body.

The lungs are not just organs.

They are living scrolls of worship—unrolling praise with every breath.

The Heart: The Altar of Rhythm

The heart is central—not geographically, but spiritually.

- It pumps 100,000 times per day.
- It sends life to every organ.
- It sings in frequencies, measurable and unique to each person.

But it is also emotional.

The Bible says:

> *"Out of the abundance of the heart, the mouth speaks."*
> *— Matthew 12:34*

Leonardo understood the mechanics of the heart—but also its meaning.

It is:

- A chamber of covenant.
- A vessel of virtue.
- A drum of divine memory.

Modern science confirms that the heart has its own neural network—called the heart-brain—capable of remembering, learning, and leading.

The heart doesn't just beat. It remembers God.

The Stomach and Gut: The Second Mind

The stomach and intestines contain over 100 million neurons—earning it the title, "the second brain."

Why does this matter?

Because:

- Discernment lives here.
- Conviction starts here.
- Gut feelings are often prophetic—not emotional, but somatic truth.

Leonardo may not have known neurology, but he placed detailed attention on the gut—sketching its folds, texture, and structure.

In scripture, the belly is often the seat of emotion and spirit:

> *"Out of your belly shall flow rivers of living water."*
>
> *—John 7:38*

The stomach processes physical food, yes—but it also processes emotional and spiritual weight.

You don't just think with your brain. You perceive with your gut.

Bones, Ligaments, Tendons: The Frame of Truth

Bones are not dead. They are:

- Living tissue
- Capable of healing
- Resonant with sound (bone conduction)

Ezekiel 37:

> *"Can these dry bones live?"*

God breathes, and the bones rattle, reconnect, reform— until the body stands again.

The skeletal system in Vitruvian Man is the geometry of resurrection.

- Ligaments hold like covenants.
- Tendons pull like obedience.
- Joints move like grace—enabling flexibility without fracture.

Your skeleton is not just structure.

It is a song of surrender and strength.

The Spine: The Scroll of Light The spine:

- Holds 33 vertebrae.
- Encases the spinal cord.
- Stretches from brain to pelvis.

It is the pillar of fire within man. In temple design:

- The menorah (seven-branched lampstand) stood as a central light source.
- The spine, with its seven major vertebral groupings, reflects this divine lamp.

Each vertebra is like:

- A scroll segment
- A musical note
- A stepping stone between earth and mind

The spine preaches verticality.

That your walk should lead upward.

It holds you erect—not by force, but by divine sequencing.

The Brain: The Holy of Holies

Finally, we arrive at the brain—the seat of consciousness.

Leonardo mapped its outer lobes, ventricles, and folds with precision.

But what science is just now beginning to understand is what scripture already told us:

- The mind is where battles are won or lost.
- The renewal of the mind leads to transformation (Romans 12:2).
- The mind of Christ is available to us (1 Corinthians 2:16).

The brain:

- Generates thought, but also receives vision.
- Stores language, but also hosts revelation.
- Organizes memory, but also reflects eternity.

And at its center lies:

- The pineal gland, long called the "seat of the soul."
- The corpus callosum, the bridge between left (logic) and right (creativity).

The brain is not a throne of reason. It is a temple of illumination.

Final Benediction: The Body as Sermon

You are not just a person. You are a parable.

Not just made—but proclaimed.

Each part of your body is:

- A letter in a divine language
- A note in a sacred song
- A measure in the math of the Messiah.

Leonardo sketched it.

You embody it.

The eye sees.

The ear hears.

The jaw speaks.

The lungs breathe.

The heart beats.

The bones stand.

The brain receives.

The body reveals.

You are the living Word.

"The head holds more than the mind – it holds the mystery. Thought may govern, but it is worship that crowns."

Damiano B. Centola

STEP SEVEN
The Human Head – The Seat of Thought, Will, and Worship

Chapter VII

The Heart and the Sacred Rhythm

"Before your mouth ever spoke, your heart had already started singing."
—Writer Damiano B. Centola

The First Sound in the Womb

Before you saw, spoke, or touched the world you pulsed.
Around 22 days after conception, before the brain is fully formed, before your limbs grow, your heart begins to beat.
Why?
Because rhythm is the first language of life.
Leonardo da Vinci believed the heart was not merely a pump, but a sacred engine—a living metronome synchronizing man to the rhythm of the cosmos.

Four Chambers, One Covenant

The human heart is divided into four chambers:

- Right Atrium
- Right Ventricle
- Left Atrium
- Left Ventricle

And yet—one unified beat.

In Hebrew numerology, four represents creation:

- Four elements: earth, water, fire, air
- Four directions: north, south, east, west
- Four rivers of Eden
- Four Gospels

The four chambers are not mechanical—they are liturgical. Each beat is:

- An act of giving (systole)
- An act of receiving (diastole)

Like prayer. Like worship. Like covenant. Your heart is not just made to live—It is made to commune.

The Pulse: Divine Rhythm in Flesh

The average human heart beats 100,000 times per day. That's over 35 million times per year.

And yet…

- Each beat is unique to you.
- Your heart rate changes with thought, touch, and even memory.
- Music and scripture affect its rhythm. Why?

Because the heart is not just physical. It is responsive.

David said:

> *"My heart is steadfast, O God, my heart is steadfast; I will sing and make melody."*
> *—Psalm 57:7*

What does it mean to have a steadfast heart? A heart that:

- Keeps beat under pressure.
- Worships in rhythm with Heaven.
- Refuses to break rhythm even when bruised.

The devil attacks rhythm. But God restores tempo.

The Electric Symphony

The heart runs on bioelectricity

Each beat is triggered by the sinoatrial (SA) node, often called the natural pacemaker.

It creates an electrical impulse, which:

- Moves through your heart muscle
- Contracts the atria and ventricles
- Sends blood through the body

But this current can be measured. It's called an ECG (electrocardiogram).

That means:

- Your rhythm is traceable
- Your frequency is recordable
- Your life is a literal waveform

GOLDEN SPIRALS IN YOUR DNA

Ever wonder if life's code has a divine beat? Let's dive in.

Cycle ≈ 34 Å
Diameter ≈ 21 Å

The DNA helix? Its cycle is 34 angstroms, diameter 21 ~ Fibonacci numbers. Their ratio, $34/21 \approx 1.619$ mirrors the golden ratio, $\varphi = 1.618$

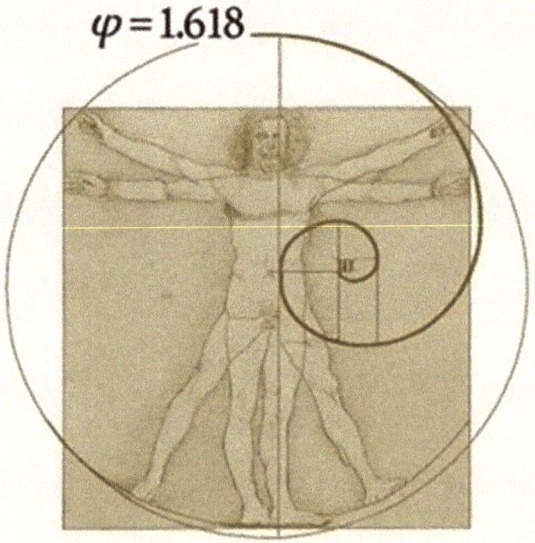

The breath of God curling our code!

Damiano B. Centola.

You are made in the image of a God who said, "Let there be light."

And your heart answers with waves of energy.

The Heart-Brain: Your Inner Oracle

Science now confirms that the heart has its own neural network:

- Over 40,000 neurons
- Capable of learning, feeling, and remembering

The heart sends more signals to the brain than the brain sends to the heart. Let that settle in.

Your emotional intelligence, your discernment, your intuition—all begin in the chest.

The seat of wisdom is not the skull.

It is the sacred muscle that bleeds, forgives, and praises. The Heart as Altar and Scroll

In both the Old and New Testaments, the heart is not a symbol of emotion—but of covenant:

- Psalm 119:11 — "I have hidden Your word in my heart…"
- Jeremiah 31:33 — "I will write My law upon their hearts."
- Hebrews 10:16 — "I will put My laws into their hearts, and in their minds will I write them."

That means:

- The Heart is not just a pump.
- It is a scroll.
- And God writes His name on it. Leonardo drew anatomy.

But the Holy Spirit writes identity.

Broken Hearts Still Beat

A heart can be:

- Strong, and still bruised.
- Holy, and still broken.
- Wounded, and still worshipping.

This is the mystery of God:

"The Lord is close to the brokenhearted."
—Psalm 34:18

Even when fractured, the rhythm continues.

Because the heart doesn't just respond to life—it anchors it.

The Crucified Heart

At Calvary, Christ's side was pierced. From His heart came:

- Water — symbolic of cleansing
- Blood — symbolic of covenant

The Church was born from the side of Christ.

Just as Eve was drawn from the side of Adam.

The cross is:

- A vertical beam (Heaven to earth)
- A horizontal beam (man to man)
- And at its center—His heart

The rhythm stopped once… so that ours would beat forever.

Musical Notes, Blood Flow, and Heaven's Meter

Leonardo played the lyre, and saw music in everything. He noted that the rhythms of the body follow:

- The beat of the heart
- The flow of the breath
- The patterns of natural tempo

Modern research confirms:

- Heart rate entrains to music
- Certain keys and tempos stabilize cardiac rhythm
- Gregorian chants, Hebrew psalms, even 432Hz music lower blood pressure

The heart listens to Heaven.

Music doesn't just move it—it reminds it of its source.

Final Reflection:

The Pulse Is the Voice Leonardo drew a man within a circle and square.

He made measurements from the navel, from the limbs, from the head.

But perhaps the true center is what he couldn't draw. The heart.

It:

- Connects mind to spirit
- Bridges blood and breath
- Holds memory, covenant, love

Your heart is the center not of shape, but of song. You are not simply alive. You are singing.

Every beat says:

I am created.

I am loved.

I am purposed.

I am echoing God.

GOLDEN SPIRALS IN YOUR DNA

Ever wonder if life's code has a divine beat?

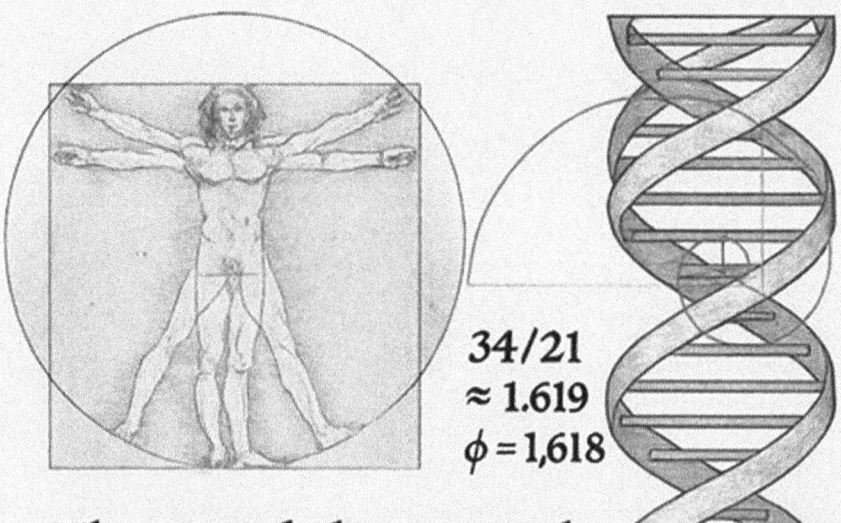

34/21
≈ 1.619
ϕ = 1,618

The DNA helix? Its cycle is 34 angstroms, its diameter 21~ both Fibonacci numbers.

Their ratio mirrors the golden ratio…

The breath of God curling our code!

Damiano B. Centola.

Damiano B. Centola

Spiraled into Being

Spiraled into Being

(A Fibonacci Poem by Damiano B. Centola)

1   Born—

1   Alone—

2   He breathed. Light stirred—

3   Time unfurled. Dust danced—

5   A whisper spiraled through clay—

8   Hands shaped math into skin, into soul—

13   The code within us curved like prayer
in breath—

21   From rib to root, from thought to flame,
His pattern repeats—

34   In seashells, storms, galaxies, leaves,
bloodlines—He speaks again—

55   Not in thunder, but in ratios of beauty,
where silence counts the stars—

89   We are not random. We are not accidents.
We are echo, equation, eternity.

144   This is the breath of the Divine—written
not just in scripture, but in spiral.

Damiano B. Centola

'Leonardo drew flesh—but hinted at glory. The body is a veil, and light is waiting behind it.'

Damiano B. Centola

STEP EIGHT
The Veil Between Body and Glory – Clothed in Light

DAMIANO B. CENTOLA

Chapter VIII

Breath, Bone, and Body as Scroll

"You were written before you were born. Your body is the parchment. Your breath is the ink."
—*Writer Damiano B. Centola*

The Body as a Living Scroll

Leonardo da Vinci measured the body to define its dimensions.
But what if the body is not just measured? What if it is meant to be read?
In biblical tradition:

- Scrolls were made of animal skin (parchment)
- Ink was applied by scribes who understood holy placement
- Scrolls were unrolled, not flipped—revealed over time

You too, are unrolled.

- From womb to breath
- From form to fullness
- From bone to word

The body is not a diagram. It is scripture in motion.

Breath: The First and Final Stroke

Genesis 2:7 says:

> *"Then the LORD God formed man of the dust of the ground, and breathed into his nostrils the breath of life..."*

Before man spoke, before man moved, he was breathed upon.

That breath:

- Gave animation
- Gave identity
- Gave speech

In Hebrew, the word ruach means:

- Breath
- Wind
- Spirit

And in Greek: pneuma

You are not a machine powered by oxygen.

You are a scroll activated by divine breath.

Every inhale is a signature. Every exhale, a sending.

The Bone: The Framework of Testimony

Bones are not lifeless.

They:

- Produce blood (in the marrow)
- Store memory (trauma and healing)
- Preserve identity (DNA)

In Ezekiel 37, God tells the prophet:

> *"Prophesy to these bones... and they shall live."*

And the bones respond.

They rattle.

They connect. They rise.

The human skeleton, when viewed head-on, is symmetrical.

- Spine as scroll
- Ribs as pages
- Skull as seal

You are a book written in bone.

Leonardo's skeletal sketches show precision, but they miss purpose—

until the bones are seen as divine sentence structure.

The Skin: The Covering and the Veil

Skin is your first language—the sense of touch.

It is also:
- A boundary
- A canvas
- A veil

Like the veil of the temple, skin:

- Covers sacred space
- Can be pierced
- Can be anointed

In Leviticus, the priest anointed the ear, thumb, and big toe.

These represent hearing, doing, and walking.

The skin is symbolic of:

- Your testimony
- Your transformation
- Your story seen from the outside

The skin is not just fabric. It is evidence of your scroll.

The Blood: The Living Ink

The blood:

- Carries oxygen, like breath
- Delivers nutrients, like truth
- Records genetic code, like memory. Blood flows in rhythm, in circuits, in language.

In Exodus 12, the blood on the doorpost was a sign—a written mark of protection.

In the New Covenant, Christ's blood becomes:

- The seal of redemption
- The ink of eternal life

Leonardo drew the vascular system as rivers of life. But we now know:

- Each blood cell has a lifespan
- Each carries the record of you

You are not simply full of blood. You are written in blood.

The Spine: The Scroll Unrolling

Your spine contains 33 vertebrae—a number rich in symbolism:

- Christ lived 33 years
- The spine connects brain to body
- It houses the spinal cord—your internal messenger

The spine unrolls as:

- A Torah scroll
- A ladder (Jacob's Ladder)
- A highway of light

Each vertebra is like a verse, supporting the next. Break the scroll, and you cannot stand.

Strengthen it, and you walk upright.

Tendons and Ligaments: Divine Grammar

Tendons connect muscle to bone Ligaments connect bone to bone.

They are not glamorous. They are grammar. Without them, you have:

- No structure
- No meaning

No movement In spiritual terms:

- Tendons are faith (that connects effort to identity)
- Ligaments are truth (that holds everything together)

Paul writes:

> *"From Him the whole body… held together by every supporting*
> *ligament…"*
> *—Ephesians 4:16*

Leonardo's precision in sketching tendons shows he knew—
these unseen parts bind the body to its story.

The Tongue: The Quill of God

No part of the body is more powerful—and more dangerous. Proverbs 18:21:

> *"Death and life are in the power of the tongue…"*

The tongue:

- Speaks creation
- Names identity
- Declares destiny

In the scroll of the body, the tongue is the pen.

Leonardo studied its muscles.

We now know:

- It's the only muscle anchored at one end
- It moves across borders (taste, speech, worship)

It's your signature organ.

When you speak, you write. When you lie, you erase. When you praise,

you inscribe Heaven.

The Breath of Christ and the Sealed Scroll

In John 20:22:

> *"He breathed on them and said, 'Receive the Holy Spirit.'"*

And in Revelation 5:

- There is a sealed scroll in Heaven.
- No one can open it.
- Until the Lamb appears
- Then the scroll is opened.
- You are that scroll.
- You are the body He breathed on.
- You are the one He sealed with His Spirit.

The Vitruvian Man is not only a design.

He is a manuscript of glory.

Final Benediction: You Are the Message

You are not random.

You are not ink spilled.

You are ink intended.

You are not tissue in time.

You are:

- Written by the breath of God
- Structured in sacred form
- Read by angels and demons alike
- Declared by the Creator as good

Leonardo drew the perfect man. But you are not just drawn. You are authored.

And every line, every organ, every pulse says:

> *"He who measured the heavens first measured himself."*
>
> —*Writer Damiano B. Centola*

Leonardo did not just draw a man— he drew Adam waiting for Christ, and Christ preparing the temple of man.

Damiano B. Centola

STEP NINE
The Male Form – Adam, Christ and the Final Temple

DAMIANO B. CENTOLA

DAMIANO B. CENTOLA

Chapter IX

The Temple of Man

"He did not dwell in temples made by hands, because He was fashioning a greater temple—you."
—Writer Damiano B. Centola

The Architecture of Holiness

God has always been an architect.

- In Exodus 25–40, He gives Moses precise blueprints for the Tabernacle.
- In 1 Kings 6, Solomon constructs the temple with sacred measurements.
- In Ezekiel 40–48, a future Temple is revealed in prophetic vision.
- And in 1 Corinthians 3:16, Paul declares: "Do you not know that you are God's temple and that God's Spirit dwells in you?"

Temples are not metaphorical. They are literal, spatial, and sacred.

Leonardo's Vitruvian Man—arms outstretched; body centered—was not just mathematical.

It was priestly.

The human form is not random.

It is a tabernacle of transcendence.

Outer Court – The Body and Its Boundaries

In the Tabernacle:

The Outer Court was visible, open, and active.

Here, sacrifices were made.

Here, washing occurred in the bronze laver.

In the body:

The skin, limbs, and organs form this outer space. It is where we labor, serve, and move.

Your body is your Outer Court.

It is the space where you interact with the world. The hands are altars.

The feet are gates.

The eyes are lamps.

And the body must be cleansed, consecrated, and aligned.

The Inner Court – The Soul and Its Purpose

The Inner Court contained:

- The Table of Showbread (provision)
- The Altar of Incense (prayer)
- The Lampstand (illumination)

In the body:

- The soul hosts these same elements.

Table of Showbread ☐ Stomach/Gut

It digests not only food, but emotion, intuition, and conviction.

Altar of Incense ☐ Lungs/Breath

Every breath becomes prayer when aligned with divine rhythm.

Lampstand ☐ Mind/Consciousness

The brain, with its billions of neurons, reflects the sevenfold light of wisdom.

Your soul is the Inner Court—

where memory, longing, and love are lifted before the Lord.

The Holy of Holies – The Heart as Mercy Seat

The Holy of Holies housed:

- The Ark of the Covenant
- The Shekinah Glory
- The Mercy Seat—where God met man

Only the High Priest entered once a year, with fear and trembling. In the body, the heart is this sacred chamber.

- Hidden
- Protected by ribs (like the veil)
- Pulsing with covenant It is where:
- Blood flows like sacrifice
- Memory stores law and love
- God speaks, not in thunder, but in pulse
- Your heart is the Holy of Holies.

It is where you hear God whisper,

"You are mine."

Veils, Curtains, and Skin

The Tabernacle was separated by veils:

- Outer veil
- Inner veil
- Veil before the Ark Your body, too, has layers:
- Skin
- Fascia
- Membranes between bone and blood

Christ's crucifixion tore the veil from top to bottom.
That veil symbolized the separation between God and man.
But after Calvary:

- The veil became your skin
- The temple became your body

Access was granted—not to a place, but to a person.

Measurements and Sacred Math

The Tabernacle was constructed with:

- Exact cubits
- Golden ratios
- Layered symmetry

Leonardo's Vitruvian Man is also built on these principles:

- Centered on the navel (source of life)
- Encased in a circle (eternity) and square (earthly dominion)
- Limbs extended in perfect proportions. The man becomes the temple.

You are built to host the Holy.
Every measurement of you is intentional.

Priestly Garments and Identity

The High Priest wore:

- A breastplate with 12 stones
- Linen garments without seam

A turban with the phrase:

"HOLY TO THE LORD"

You, too, wear garments:

- Skin as robe
- Blood as anointing
- Breath as incense

And your name is written where?

Not on garments, but on the Lamb's Book of Life Leonardo gave us the outline.

Christ gives us the indwelling.

The Glory Within

In the Tabernacle, when construction was complete:

"Then the cloud covered the tent of meeting, and the glory of the

LORD filled the tabernacle."

—Exodus 40:34

You are not just body. You are not just soul. You are Spirit-filled.

And when your design is aligned with Heaven—The glory descends. Not as a cloud over a building. But as a fire within your chest.

You are the temple of the Living God. And your heart is the throne.

Final Benediction:

The Architecture of You;

You are:

- Designed with purpose
- Measured with precision
- Anointed with Spirit You are:
- Altar and priest
- Sacrifice and sanctuary
- Holy of Holies and flame of worship

Leonardo gave the world the drawing. God gave the world you. You are the temple not made with hands.

And the world will never be the same once you understand what you carry.

"Man was not
drawn to be
admired, but
to be decoded.
For hidden in
his measure is
the Name
above all names."

Damiano B. Centola

STEP TEN
The Completion – Man, Creation,
and the Hidden Name of God

DAMIANO B. CENTOLA

Chapter X
The Final Unveiling — Man as Messenger

"Design is not the end. It is the voice. You were not made to be admired. You were made to be heard."
—*Writer Damiano B. Centola*

The Messenger Emerges from the Design

Leonardo drew the perfect man—centered, extended, encased in circle and square.

But the final purpose of such a figure is not symmetry. It is speech.

It is message.

It is revelation.

Throughout this book we have uncovered:

- The frame (Chapter 1)
- The center (Chapter 2)
- The double posture (Chapter 3)
- The sacred lines (Chapters 4–9)

But what good is a design if it says nothing?

You were not made to be studied.

You were made to speak for the One who designed you.

The Divine Logic of the Body

The Greek word logos means:

- Word
- Reason

Principle In John 1:1:

> *"In the beginning was the Word (Logos), and the Word was with*
> *God, and the Word was God."*

You are made in the image of the Logos. That means you carry reason.

But more than that—you carry message.

Your:

- Eyes observe
- Ears discern
- Tongue declares
- Hands write
- Feet go
- Skin feels
- Heart remembers

All coordinated as a single communication system.

The body is not only architecture.

It is an alphabet of the eternal.

The Voice of Man in the Cosmos

Why did God breathe into Adam?

Why not simply spark him into life?

Because breath is voice in waiting.

You are the only species on earth with:

- Abstract speech
- Spiritual language
- Moral reasoning
- Praise

When Leonardo drew the Vitruvian Man.

He captured the moment where man:

- Stands still like stone
- But also reaches like flame

You are statue and prophet. You are dust and declaration.
The stars declare His glory. But man speaks it.

From Drawing to Destiny

The Vitruvian Man is not finished. He is paused Leonardo left him:

- With arms raised
- Legs parted
- Eyes forward Why?

Because he was never meant to remain on the page.
He was drawn to be sent.
Vitruvian symmetry is preparation for apostolic action.
You are not just a design. You are destined.

The Messenger as Witness

Isaiah 43:10:

> *"You are My witnesses," declares the LORD.*

The body testifies:

- In suffering
- In glory
- In motion
- In stillness Every:
  - Scar becomes scripture
  - Stretch becomes symbolism
  - Stumble becomes testimony You were made to:
  - Speak wisdom
  - Walk in power
  - Reveal the invisible through the visible

You are God's scroll in the marketplace His geometry in the chaos
His message in the flesh.

Divine Messenger, Global Reach

Science has reached the quantum. Mathematics the infinite.

Art the sublime.

But none of these alone speak God's full language.

Only one creature can:

- Paint
- Calculate
- Worship
- Pray
- Cry
- Create Only man.

Leonardo pointed us toward the possibility. But only the Spirit fulfills it.

You are the synthesis of:

- Heaven and Earth
- Thought and flame
- Blueprint and breath

The mystery is no longer hidden. It is alive in you.

The Mouthpiece of Heaven

The prophet Jeremiah said:

> *"Your words were found, and I ate them, and Your word was to me
> the joy and rejoicing of my heart."*

Ezekiel was commanded:

> *"Eat this scroll, and go speak..."*

You are not only a scroll.

You are the mouthpiece of what you carry.

That's why the design matters. That's why the math matters.

Because message without design is noise. And design without message is vanity. But when the two meet— You become truth in motion.

Final Benediction:

You Are the Mystery Made Known.

The square and circle could not contain you.

The ink of Leonardo could not finish you.

The canvas of the world cannot explain you.

Because you are:

- A vessel of divine breath
- A harmony of sacred measures
- A witness to the eternal Artist

> *"He who measured the heavens first measured himself."*
>
> —*Writer Damiano B. Centola*

You are:

- The design
- The scroll
- The sanctuary
- The message

Now go.

Let your words be measured.

Let your walk be holy.

Let your posture echo eternity.

Let the world behold the Messenger— Drawn by God, measured in grace, Unveiled in power.

She is not
measured by
symmetry
alone,
but by the echo
of heaven
hidden in her
frame.

Her curves
were not drawn
for function—
but for the
music of form,
the breath
of beginnings.

DAMIANO B.
CENTOLA

Chapter XI

Heaven's Proportions in Woman

"She is not a shadow of man—she is the echo of eternity, the crown of creation, the song in the structure."
—*Writer Damiano B. Centola*

The Missing Drawing

Leonardo never drew the Vitruvian Woman.

And that absence is deafening.

He, the master of form and beauty, rendered man in full cosmic proportion.

Yet left no geometric woman behind.

Why?

Perhaps because the feminine form refused to be boxed. Not by square.

Not by circle.

Not by compass or caliper.

Woman is not defined by boundary—she is defined by response.

Where man is frame, she is flow.

Where man is measured, she is mystery revealed in motion.

Man is declaration. Woman is song.

Genesis and the Sacred Sequence

Genesis 2:22:

> *"Then the LORD God made a woman from the rib He had taken out*
> *of the man…"*

The Hebrew word used is "banah", meaning:

- To build
- To architect
- To craft intricately

Man was formed. Woman was built.

A difference in purpose, not in value.

She was not made from dust—She was made from a living rhythm.

From rib, near the heart.

This was not accident. The rib:

- Protects the heart
- Expands with breath
- Wraps the voice

The woman was designed from what sings.

Her creation is not less—it is closer to the breath of God.

The Geometry of Grace

Leonardo's proportions in man are sharp— Angles, bones, alignment.

But in woman:

- The lines become curves
- The corners become chambers
- The stance becomes invitation

The hip-to-waist ratio of ideal health in woman (0.7) is not only
aesthetic:

- It reflects fertility
- It mirrors the golden mean
- It appears in music, light, galaxies

The womb itself sits at the golden intersection of the female frame. The female pelvis is circular—not angular. To carry life, not geometry. She is not made for the drawing. She is made for the dance of design.

Woman as Tabernacle In the temple:

The Holy of Holies was enclosed, guarded, sacred.
So too, the woman's womb:

- Hidden
- Holy
- Unseen by man, but known by God
- The uterus, shaped like a shofar, echoes with:

    ➢ The voice of creation

    ➢ The trumpet of life

    ➢ The opening of the scroll

Her cycle reflects the moons.
Her blood is not a wound—it is offering.
Woman is the only being whose internal altar renews itself with time. She is not secondary.
She is temple within temple.

The Voice, the Face, the Flame

The female voice:

- Resonates in higher frequencies
- Has greater emotional tone
- Was created to soothe and summon
- It is the echo of Eden.

Her face:

- More symmetrical on average
- Designed to reflect both strength and softness

She is not a contradiction—She is coexistence perfected.
She is the fire that warms, And the water that quenches.
She is the song of symmetry, where mathematics meets miracle.

Mary: The Arc of Womanhood

When God chose to enter the world, He did not come through:

- Temple
- Throne
- Sword

He came through a woman. Luke 1:38:

> *"Behold, I am the servant of the Lord; let it be to me according to*
> *your word."*

She became:

- Ark of the New Covenant
- Living tabernacle
- The only human to carry God inside her body

Mary is not only a figure of faith—She is a divine endorsement of woman's design.

She is:

- Humble and glorious
- Grounded and exalting
- A teenage girl… and Heaven's gateway

The Final Equation: Flame + Form = Woman

Where man may be:

- Compass
- Hammer
- Declaration

Woman is:

- Lyre
- Flame
- Benediction Together:
- They form the full image of God.
- They represent Spirit and Word, Truth and Beauty, Wisdom and Power.

But alone?

She needs no apology. She stands:

- In balance
- In breath
- In unmeasurable elegance

She is the proportion not meant to be drawn— Only encountered.

Final Benediction:

She Is the Hidden Glory

She is:

- The chamber of life
- The scroll of breath
- The tabernacle of mystery She is:
- Not a revision
- Not a reflection
- But a revelation

She walks in golden rhythm. She speaks with heavenly tone. She carries the proportion of paradise.

She is woman—The missing Vitruvian.

The mystery that completes the circle.

HEAVEN'S PROPORTION IN WOMEN

The sacred code
was not carved
in the womb,
but curled around it—
like a whisper.

He placed the spiral
within her—
not for science
to name,
but for the
heavens to echo.

— DAMIANO B.
CENTOLA

Chapter XII

The Geometry of Resurrection — From Dust to Glory; Beyond the Drawing: Da Vinci, DNA, and the Divine Future

"He saw the shape. Now we see the code."
— Writer Damiano B. Centola

Da Vinci's Obsession with the Invisible

Leonardo da Vinci's notebooks reveal a singular obsession:
How does the visible body conceal the invisible soul? By candlelight, he dissected over thirty corpses— Seeking the secrets of life hidden beneath the skin.
He sketched.

- Arteries like rivers
- Muscles like ropes
- Joints like hinges in sacred machines

But what he could not touch was what held it all together: DNA.
And yet—he hinted at it. The spiral of the intestine, The coiled cochlea of the ear, The swirling heart's vortex… These weren't accidents.
They were whispers of the spiral to come. Precursors to the double helix.

The Divine Double Helix

DNA—Deoxyribonucleic Acid

3 billion letters. 23 paired chromosomes.

Shaped like a spiral ladder of life.

Its language?

A repeating sequence of four bases:

A, T, C, G.

A code written into every cell.

Not just biological instruction.

But divine inscription.

> *"All the days ordained for me were written in Your book before one*
> *of them came to be."*
> *-- Psalm 139:16*

God didn't only write it in Heaven— He wrote it in you. DNA is not just data.

It is covenant. It is scroll. It is signature.

The Spiral as Signature

The spiral is not unique to DNA. It shows up in:

- Galaxies
- Seashells
- Tornadoes
- Fingerprints

The Fibonacci sequence—1, 1, 2, 3, 5, 8, 13…—is the mathematics of divine recurrence.

And within the human body:

- Joints rotate like spiral gears
- The cochlea curves to perfect sound
- Hair follicles, spinal alignment, even heart flow—all spiral with intent

Leonardo's Vitruvian Man appears still—yet within him, the divine spiral turns.

He is drawn by geometry. But he is animated by glory.

From Geometry to Genome

Leonardo measured limbs from the navel.

We now measure chromosomes from the centromere.

He mapped:

- Proportions of limbs
- The curve of the skull
- Ratios of torso to leg Today, we map:
- Genomes
- Epigenetic memories
- CRISPR edits

What we find isn't chaos. We find pattern.

We find:

- Symmetry
- Rhythm
- Sequence
- Harmony

Science is not separate from Spirit. God didn't stop writing in scripture. He continued in cells.

Divine Identity in the Age of Machines

As AI, robotics, and biotechnology rise, the question resurfaces:

What is man?

If we can:

- Replicate limbs
- Edit DNA
- Simulate intelligence

Then what remains sacred? Breath.

No algorithm can create a soul. No machine can carry eternity.

Man is more than material.

He is the messenger—Vitruvian and vertical.

Earthbound…yet eternal.

The Promise Hidden in the Bones

Bones are not just scaffolding. They are scrolls.
Inside them:

- Marrow composes blood
- Calcium stores memory
- Symmetry whispers of design

Even when man returns to dust, his bones remain. Why?
Because bones prophesy.

"Can these bones live?"
"Prophesy to the bones..."
(Ezekiel 37)

When God breathes—bones align. Structure becomes soul again.
Your geometry was never just to hold you up— It was to hold a promise.

The Seed and the Shape

"The body that is sown is perishable, it is raised imperishable..."
-- 1 Corinthians 15:42-44

Paul called the body a seed.
This means:

- What dies is not what rises
- But what dies contains what will rise

Your body carries the blueprint for your resurrected form:

- The square: earthly boundaries
- The circle: eternal destiny

The center:

- Christ in you, the hope of glory "The Vitruvian Man" is the seed.
- The Resurrected Man is the Tree of Life.

Light Replaces Shadow

In this world, the body casts shadow. In resurrection—it will cast light.

> *"Then the righteous will shine like the stars..."*

Daniel 12:3

Your new form will be:

- Recognizable
- Radiant
- Recalibrated No more:
- Decay
- Disease
- Division between soul and form

The body will not be a container— It will be a covenant of light.

The Mathematics of Immortality.

The golden ratio (1.618) governs:

- Hurricanes
- Seashells
- Spiral galaxies
- Your face, your limbs, your heart

In resurrection:

- Ratios are no longer bound by entropy
- Time no longer erodes design
- Geometry no longer decays—it glorifies Imagine:
- Bones transfigured into radiant beams
- Blood replaced with rivers of living water
- Skin clothed in incorruptible flame

The resurrection is not only spiritual— It is mathematical fire.

The Breath Returns

Genesis begins with breath

John ends with Christ breathing:

> *"Receive the Holy Spirit."*
>
> *--John 20:22*

Between those breaths, man weeps, laughs, and sings. But in glory?

Every breath becomes praise. Every inhalation—eternity. Every exhale —divine echo.

The Body Beyond Gravity Christ rose with:

- Wounds still visible
- Eyes like fire
- Power to vanish and appear

He ate… and walked through walls. He bore scars… and bore light. This is not myth. It is prototype.

> *"He will transform our lowly bodies so they will be like His glorious body."*
>
> *--Philippians 3:21*

Resurrected humanity is not angelic. It is upgraded. Fully human— yet remade in divinity.

From Vitruvian to Victorious

Leonardo's man stood:

- Naked
- Reaching
- Balanced in tension

The resurrected man will stand:

- Clothed in light
- Rooted in truth
- Crowned in glory

His pose shifts—from reaching to reigning.
From balance to benediction.

Leonardo's Prophetic Shadow

Da Vinci drew parachutes, planes, submarines— centuries before their creation.

Was he guessing… or glimpsing?

The Vitruvian Man is not just past—he is future. Leonardo placed man:

- Inside a square (Earth)
- Inside a circle (Heaven) What if:
- The square is science
- The circle is spirit
- And man—the bridge?

You are not stuck between eras. You are the convergence of them.

The Future Human: A Temple of Light

Revelation 21 describes the city of God:

- Formed in gold
- Measured in cubits
- Lit not by sun, but by the Lamb

This is not digital destiny. It is divine architecture. The resurrected man is not cybernetic.

He is eternal, glorious, proportioned by Heaven.

"For this perishable body must put on the imperishable..."

--1 Corinthians 15:53

Final Benediction: From Dust to Glory

He who measured the stars… measured you.

He who traced the galaxies… traced your soul.

You will rise:
- Not only in spirit—but in structure
- Not only by grace—but by fulfilled geometry
- The Vitruvian Man ends in ink.

But you—You will rise in fire.

You are:
- Scroll and flame
- Seed and song
- Dust… and divine destiny

From dust to glory—The design is complete.

"The same God who measured your bones in the womb will remap

them in glory."

—Writer Damiano B. Centola

Chapter XIII

Epilogue: When the Drawing Speaks; The Line, the Breath, and the Flame

"We were never meant to be flat on parchment. We were meant to rise—alive, luminous, infinite."
—Writer Damiano B. Centola

The Silence After the Ink

There is a kind of silence that arrives not with absence, but with completion.

The silence after the last brushstroke. The pause after the last chisel strike.

The moment when the artist steps back—not unsure, but undone by what has emerged.

This is that moment.

Leonardo da Vinci set his ink to parchment in 1490, drawing not just a man, but a message encoded in the geometry of being. And for centuries, that drawing sat still.

Staring. Waiting.

It wasn't just asking to be observed, it was waiting to be answered.

Today, the drawing has found its voice. And it speaks through you.

From Flat to Full

We began in a square.

We passed through the circle.

We studied the limbs, the ratios, the breath, the bones.

But what we uncovered wasn't just proportion— it was prophecy. We peeled back ink and anatomy to find the whisper of God.

We traced the navel to find the center of all things.

We followed spirals in DNA to uncover the alphabet of creation.

We stood at the threshold of mathematics and found ourselves face-to-face with mystery.

What Da Vinci only hinted at with compass and caliper, God has now revealed with Spirit and fire.

You were never just a sketch. You were always a scroll.

The Body Was Always a Message

Every feature of the Vitruvian Man speaks— if you know how to listen.

The dual poses whisper of dual nature: Stillness and motion.

Earth and spirit.

The present man and the future one.

The limbs extended toward the square proclaim:

"I was born in boundary."

But the limbs reaching into the circle declare:

"I was made for eternity."

You were not created simply to survive within form.

You were created to transcend through design.

Every inch of your body speaks in divine grammar.

The ears are spiraled to receive revelation.

The heart is chambered like a temple. The hands are tools of covenant. The breath is rhythm. The bones are lines.

The soul is fire waiting to take form. This is not metaphor. This is Messiah-etched mathematics.

When Art Becomes Flesh

Leonardo never finished some of his greatest paintings. He abandoned brush for bone, paint for pulse.

He went deeper—and in doing so, he gave us something prophetic:

The body as sacred composition.

And now we stand on the other side of centuries, holding in our hands the tools he could only dream of— tools not made of wood and steel, but of truth and Spirit.

His art was a prelude. Yours is the incarnation.

The canvas has become skin.

The geometry has taken on glory.

The Drawing in the Mirror

Most people think the Da Vinci Code was a puzzle— a sequence of clues. But the real code was simpler, more silent, more scandalous:

It was you.

The geometry of God was not hidden in secret vaults.

It was embedded in the bone, traced into your fingertips, echoed in the curvature of your spine.

What Da Vinci captured in ideal form; you now carry in living function.

And when you stand before a mirror— eyes open, heart humble, breath steady— you are not just seeing reflection.

You are seeing revelation.

You are what the drawing was waiting for.

Breath, Bone, and Becoming

The Hebrew word for breath—ruach— means breath, wind, and spirit all at once.

In Genesis, God breathed and man became a living soul.

In John, Jesus breathed and said,

"Receive the Holy Spirit."

Breath is more than air.

It is the invisible signature of God.

When you inhale, you echo Eden.

When you exhale, you participate in Pentecost.

Your ribs expand like the wings of an altar. Your lungs unfurl like ancient scrolls.

You don't just breathe oxygen— you breathe origin. And one day, you will breathe eternity.

The Mystery That Moves

The Vitruvian Man appears static.

Lines fixed. Limbs pinned. A man frozen in divine geometry. But what if it was never meant to be still?

What if the drawing was always meant to move? To awaken? To evolve into incarnation?

The truth is: you are the animated version of what Leonardo saw. He drew it once.

God is drawing it now—through you. With every step you take, the circle turns.

With every gesture of love, the square expands. With every act of faith, the proportions align.

You walk as a living compass, a spinning revelation.

A divine diagram in motion.

Light Behind the Lines

If we could lift the ink off the page and peel back the layers— we'd see light behind the lines.

We'd see equations that glow. Words that hum.

Coordinates that pulse like veins.

Because the body was never meant to be outlined in black. It was meant to burn in brilliance.

You were drawn in dust, yes— but destined for glory. Leonardo drew with quill and thought.

But the Holy One draws with flame and Word.

The Design That Sings

Listen closely.

The geometry sings.

Every ratio carries rhythm. Every limb echoes a cadence. Every breath carries a song of becoming.

The bones beat like drums beneath your skin.

The voice box vibrates like a sacred string.

Your joints stretch to the tempo of divine time.

You are music molded into form. You are a psalm that walks. You are worship with wrists and knees.

When you pray, you return to the center.

When you lift your hands, you redraw the sacred figure. When you love, you complete the chorus that began in Eden.

This is what it means to be human.

The Divine Curve: Woman as Revelation

Leonardo drew a man.

But what he left blank—what history often left blank— was her.

The woman.

Not as muse. Not as measure. But as mystery made flesh.

She is not the opposite of man.

She is the echo of eternity within him. Where the man reaches, she receives. Where the man extends, she enfolds.

Where he is straight—she curves like creation itself.

Her womb is not geometry—it is Genesis. Her hips are not wide—they are gateways.

Her voice is not soft—it is the sound of the scroll opening.

She is not a second thought in the divine blueprint. She is the sanctuary.

The secret chamber.

The tabernacle within the temple.

To see her in divine proportion is to see grace given breath.

Dust with Destiny

Return to the beginning. Dust.

Not worthless— but weightless. Not discarded— but designable.

God formed man from the dust of the ground. But He didn't stop there.

He breathed.

And suddenly, the dust became destiny.

The fragile became filled.

The lifeless became luminous.

Your origin was low.

But your architecture points upward.

You are not just a product of time. You are a container of eternity.

The Vitruvian Man begins with dust. But he ends in resurrection.

The Fire in the Form

Let us speak of fire.

Not the fire that consumes— but the fire that calls.

Moses heard God through flame. Elijah was taken up in fire. Tongues of fire landed on believers at Pentecost.

Fire is not just heat. It is revelation.

You carry that fire now. In your marrow. In your memory.

In your meaning.

Your bones are not waiting for decay— they're waiting for ignition.

The same God who formed your skeleton will clothe it in incorruptible flame.

> *"The same God who measured your bones in the womb will remap them in glory."*

You were not made for ash. You were made to blaze.

The Scroll Within

The ancients believed scrolls held divine messages.

Today, we know your DNA is a scroll.

But there is more.

You are not just made of language— you are meant to speak it. You are the scroll. You are the prophecy.

You are the ink and the utterance.

Every trial in your life adds another line.

Every scar becomes punctuation. Every miracle becomes illumination.

Your very body is a sacred book in motion.

Every chapter has been read by Heaven.

And now, it's being read by the world.

The Temple Walks

The tabernacle of Moses had:

- Outer courts
- Holy place
- Holy of holies So do you.

Your skin is the veil. Your breath, the incense.

Your heart—the holy of holies.

The Spirit of God does not dwell in temples made with hands—He dwells in you.

Every step you take is holy ground. Every embrace, a ritual.

Every word of love, a priestly act.

You are not simply walking the earth. You are carrying Heaven.

The Return of the Center

From the beginning of this journey, we asked: What is the center? Was it the navel? The chest? The soul?
Now we know.
The true center is not a point on the body. It is a Person. Christ is the center of all things. The center of the circle. The axis of the square.
The divine symmetry holding the soul together. He is not part of the design. He is the design.
And you—Vitruvian, vertical, vulnerable.
Are drawn into His proportions.

The End of Separation

The ancient Greeks split body from soul. Modern thinkers split reason from revelation.

We've split science from Spirit, art from theology, flesh from glory.

But no more.

This book, this journey, this unveiling— was about the great reunion.

Everything belongs.

Everything speaks.

Everything converges in the design of God.

There is no "spiritual" vs. "physical." There is no "holy" vs. "human."

There is only: designed for glory.

The body is not the enemy of the soul.

It is the instrument of its praise.

The Drawing Walks

Leonardo's ink no longer rests. It rises. The drawing has found its voice.

Its breath. Its flame.

The line moves. The body breathes.

The mystery becomes man again.

You are not the audience. You are the answer. You are not the viewer.

You are the vision.

You are not what was once drawn. You are what is now becoming.

Becoming the Message

You once thought you were reading a message. But what if the message was reading you?

What if every page you turned was a mirror inviting reflection?

What if every proportion revealed was not just math—but mandate?

This book has not been passive. It has called to you.

It has asked you to awaken.

To stand. To stretch. To speak. To become.

Not a follower of mystery— but its fulfillment.

You are not just a character in the story of creation.

You are the scroll unrolling before angels.

You are the gospel in flesh and blood.

You are the temple the prophets dreamed of.

You are the poetry carved into time.

From Reading to Rising

Now we close the book

But this is not an end. This is an ascension. You have seen your soul in geometry.

You have traced your breath back to Eden.

You have found the line of your bones in the rhythm of the Lamb's heartbeat.

And now— You rise. Not as scholar alone.

Not as artist or theologian or dreamer. You rise as witness. A witness to the divine pattern woven into the dust.

A witness to the Spirit encoded in the spiral. A witness to the Word made flesh—in you.

The Scroll Opens in the Sky

One day, Heaven will open a scroll. Not of laws. Not of stars.
But of bodies made whole.

It will not be ink on paper. It will be light in motion. And the names written inside will be the names of those who discovered they were written all along.

Names measured in mercy. Names etched in breath. Names drawn not by men, but by Majesty.

And your name—yes, your name—will be there. The same hand that sketched galaxies sketched you.

The same Voice that said "Let there be light" has whispered your proportions into being.

The Language of the Lamb

All throughout this journey, we've traced the human body to find the code.

But beyond the spiral, beyond the center, beyond the golden ratio— there is a greater code still:

The Lamb's name on your bones.

"His name shall be written on their foreheads..."
---Revelation 22:4

This is not mere symbolism. It is destiny.

The geometry of the Lamb is the final revelation.

Because in the end, the design was never just yours.

It was His image, in you.

And what rises from the drawing is not just man victorious—but God glorified in human form.

Benediction of the Boundless

You are not the end of the design.

You are the beginning of the unveiling.

The parchment fades, but the soul expands. The square is erased, but the glory remains. And now— Stand.

Reach.

Return to the mirror, not to critique, but to confirm. You are the proof.

You are the Vitruvian fulfilled. The breath reanimated.

The design resurrected.

You are not just drawn. You are destined.

You are not just measured. You are magnified.

You are not just seen. You are sent.

So go now.

Walk in golden proportion. Speak in spirals of grace.

Stretch beyond your square.

Enter your circle.

Center yourself in Christ.

Let every bone proclaim His wisdom.

Let every breath glorify His Spirit.

Let every movement redraw the mystery.

The Drawing has spoken.

And its name… is You.

"From dust to glory. From frame to flame. This is the risen geometry of man."

Illustrated Appendix

Part I — The Sacred Design

1. The Frame of the Divine

Where structure meets spirit. Why the square and circle matter more than we ever imagined.

2. The Center of All Things

Why Leonardo placed the navel at the center—and what God placed there first.

3. The Two Poses, The Two Selves

A revelation of man's duality: still and striving, temporal and eternal.

4. The Horizontal Revelation

When man stretches side to side, secrets emerge—about balance, being, and breath.

Part II — Geometry, Organ, and Revelation

5. Divine Symmetry and Sacred Math

Fibonacci, the golden ratio, and how God's logic repeats from leaf to limb.

6. **The Eyes, the Ears, the Jaw—What the Organs Preach**

Every part of your face is a sermon. Every organ is a parable.

7. **The Heart and the Sacred Rhythm**

More than a pulse. The heart holds music, memory,
and majesty.

8. **Breath, Bone, and Body as Scroll**

The bones are not dry. They are alphabet, rhythm, and promise.

Part III — The Temple and the Future

9. **The Temple of Man**

Human anatomy aligned with Solomon's Temple—holy, measured,
veiled, and glorious.

10. **The Final Unveiling — Man as Messenger**

Leonard's image was never meant to stay on paper. It was always
meant to walk.

11. **Heaven's Proportions in Woman**

She is the arc, the altar, the tabernacle of renewal. Not secondary—
sovereign.

12. **Beyond the Drawing — Da Vinci, DNA, and the Divine Future**

Science, spiral, spirit. The Vitruvian lines lead into eternity.

13. **The Geometry of Resurrection — From Dust to Glory**

The design doesn't die. It transforms. And it rises.

Epilogue

The line, the breath, and the flame—all converge into the living
revelation of man reborn.

Illustration Gallery & Captions

Art, diagrams, and scroll-worthy sacred visuals that awaken wonder.

References & Suggested Readings

Scholarly footnotes, scriptural cross-references,
and recommended texts.

Meditation on Trust, Hope, and Eternal Love

Each book reflects his mission: to awaken a generation to the reality that they were formed with purpose, inscribed with meaning, and destined for glory.

In The Mystery of Mysteries: Unveiling the Divine Code of the Vitruvian Man, Damiano offers his most ambitious and revelatory work to date—combining sacred texts, anatomical insights, and divine mathematics into a single vision: that man was not just made in God's image, but measured by His intention.

He is a lover of truth, a messenger of beauty, and a relentless seeker of the Divine.

Where others saw only sketches, Damiano saw Scripture.

Where others saw symmetry, he saw Spirit.

And now the world is beginning to see it too.

Sources, Saints, and Scholars Honored in This Work

This book stands on the shoulders of visionaries— ancient and modern, sacred and secular—who gazed into the human frame and found truth, proportion, spirit, and glory. While this work is an original revelation authored through prayer and poetic design, I gratefully acknowledge the foundations laid by those before me.

To the Architects and Artists

Vitruvius, whose De Architectura taught the world that proportion was sacred.

Leonardo da Vinci, who captured mystery in lines—and saw man not as beast, but blueprint.

Michelangelo Buonarroti, whose chisel met divine breath in stone.

To the Thinkers and Theologians

Plato, who taught us about form and the unseen ideal. Thomas Aquinas, who merged faith with reason, and mystery with logic.

C.S. Lewis, who baptized the imagination.

Hannah Arendt, whose courage examined the human condition.

Liah Greenfeld, whose insights into the soul of nations stirred my awareness of collective design.

To the Scientists and Discoverers

Gregor Mendel, who planted the first seeds of genetic truth. James Watson & Francis Crick, who mapped the double helix. Johannes Kepler, who said "Geometry is God Himself."

And all those who decoded Fibonacci spirals in shells, storms, and stars. To the Prophets and Poets Ezekiel, who spoke to dry bones.

David, whose psalms became anatomical prophecy. Parveen Shakir, Faiz Ahmed Faiz, and Robert Frost— whose pens carried soul and stillness.

To my ancestors, mentors, and teachers—both seen and unseen—thank you for passing the scroll. I am but a scribe remembering what Heaven once wrote.

—Damiano B. Centola

Footnotes

CHAPTER I: The Frame of the Divine

- Vitruvius, Marcus Pollio. De Architectura, Book III. The original Roman architect who defined human proportion in architecture, which Leonardo later visualized in the Vitruvian Man. (c. 15 BCE)
- Leonardo da Vinci, Codex Atlanticus, folio 218r. Where da Vinci famously sketched the Vitruvian Man, citing Vitruvius' writings on human proportion. (c. 1490)
- Genesis 1:27, Holy Bible (NIV). "So, God created mankind in His own image…" Used to support the theological framework for divine measurement.
- Exodus 25:9, Holy Bible (NIV). "Make this tabernacle and all its furnishings exactly like the pattern I will show you." Cited to parallel God's use of sacred measurements.
- Psalm 139:14–16, Holy Bible (NIV). David's psalm of being "fearfully and wonderfully made," foundational to spiritual anatomy.
- Stephen Greenblatt, The Swerve: How the World Became Modern. Background on Renaissance rediscovery of ancient texts, including Vitruvius. (2011, W.W. Norton)
- Werner Herzog, Cave of Forgotten Dreams. A reference to the prehistoric human urge to draw the body, even before writing. (Documentary film, 2010) Leonardo da Vinci, translated notebooks, by Jean Paul Richter.
- On Leonardo's obsession with proportion: "The human foot is a measure of six palms." (1883 edition) Plato, Timaeus. On the role of geometry in the soul and cosmos: "God used geometric forms to structure the soul of the world." (c. 360 BCE)

- Isaiah 40:12, Holy Bible (NIV). "Who has measured the waters in the hollow of His hand… or marked off the heavens with the span of His fingers?" Used in the epigraph and theme.

Chapter II: The Center of All Things

- Leonardo da Vinci, Codex Atlanticus, folio 218r. Leonardo places the navel as the geometric center of both the circle and square—defining divine proportion through the human body. (c. 1490)
- Marcus Vitruvius Pollio, De Architectura, Book III. Vitruvius writes: "The navel is naturally the exact center of the human body." This core idea fuels Leonardo's drawing. (c. 15 BCE)
- Genesis 2:7, Holy Bible (NIV). "Then the Lord God formed a man from the dust of the ground and breathed into his nostrils the breath of life." Used to establish the first divine measurement—breath to center.
- Psalm 139:13, Holy Bible (NIV). "You knit me together in my mother's womb." Tied to the navel as the place of divine connection and nourishment.
- Plato, Phaedrus. Referenced in context of divine madness and soul-centering: "The soul is like a charioteer." (c. 370 BCE)
- Michelangelo's Creation of Adam, Sistine Chapel. In visual analysis, the navel of Adam in the fresco aligns perfectly beneath God's extended finger—a symbolic center of divine-human contact. (c. 1512)
- Isaiah 49:16, Holy Bible (NIV). "See, I have engraved you on the palms of my hands." Used as poetic geometry—God's hand imprints man's design.
- Da Vinci's anatomical notes on the fetus in the womb. Leonardo was one of the first to anatomically draw the umbilical cord and note the role of the navel. (Codex Windsor, c. 1510)
- Ezekiel 16:4–6, Holy Bible (NIV). A metaphorical passage describing an abandoned child with the umbilical cord not cut—used to reflect on identity, abandonment, and divine reconnection.
- Zohar (Jewish mystical commentary), Bereshit A. "The navel is the place from which all nourishment flows into the soul." A mystical parallel to Leonardo's anatomical focus.

Chapter III: The Two Poses, The Two Selves

- Leonardo da Vinci, Codex Atlanticus, folio 218r. Da Vinci drew the Vitruvian Man with four arms and four legs to suggest dual movement—stillness and motion.
- Genesis 1:26–27, Holy Bible (NIV). "Let us make mankind in our image, in our likeness…" interpreted as divine duality (plurality within unity).
- James 1:8, Holy Bible (KJV). "A double minded man is unstable in all his ways." Quoted in reflection of man's dual internal posture.
- Hannah Arendt, The Human Condition. On the tension between being and action, especially in the public and private selves. (1958) Plato, Republic, Book IV. Describes the soul's tripartite structure—reason, spirit, and appetite—as a balance of multiple selves.
- Romans 7:15–25, Holy Bible (NIV). Paul's discourse on doing what he hates—highlighting the tension of duality in human nature.
- Leonardo's Notebooks (Richter Translation, Vol. I) Describes movement as "life's signature." Leonardo believed motion revealed truth more than form.
- Ecclesiastes 3:1–8, Holy Bible (NIV). "A time to be born and a time to die…" The poetic duality of seasons referenced in man's posture.
- Michelangelo's Slaves sculptures Incomplete figures emerging from marble—used to mirror the image of man both bound and breaking free.
- Psalm 42:5, Holy Bible (NIV). "Why, my soul, are you downcast?" A cry from the inner man—mirroring Leonardo's outer expression.

Chapter IV: The Horizontal Revelation

- Leonardo da Vinci, Vitruvian Study Notes. Horizontal lines extend from the man's outstretched arms to touch the square's edge—revealing sacred width.
- Exodus 26:15–25, Holy Bible (NIV). Horizontal boards used in the Tabernacle's structure— mirrored in the body's shoulder-to-shoulder span.
- 1 Kings 6:15–20, Holy Bible (NIV). Solomon's Temple described with horizontal paneling and inner dimensions—echoed in man's torso.

- Isaiah 53:2, Holy Bible (NIV). "He had no beauty or majesty… like a root out of dry ground." Horizontal imagery linked to humility and growth.
- Da Vinci's The Last Supper (1498) Compositionally horizontal—spiritually vertical— reflecting a divine tension between movement and message.
- Ezekiel 37:1–10, Holy Bible (NIV). "Can these bones live?"—the Valley of Dry Bones spreads horizontally, until breath enters vertically.
- Giorgio Vasari, Lives of the Artists. Describes Leonardo's obsession with width-to-height balance in human figures. (1550)
- John 19:18, Holy Bible (NIV). "There they crucified Him, and with Him two others…" Horizontal suffering with vertical redemption.
- Pythagoras, fragmentary teachings. Taught symmetry between horizontal and vertical to represent harmony of body and soul.
- Psalm 18:19, Holy Bible (NIV). "He brought me out into a spacious place…" Interpreted as divine geometry meeting spiritual expansion.

Chapter V: Divine Symmetry and Sacred Math

- Fibonacci (Leonardo of Pisa), Liber Abaci. Introduced the Fibonacci sequence (1, 1, 2, 3, 5…) to Western mathematics. (1202)
- Luca Pacioli, De Divina Proportione. Leonardo illustrated this book, which explored the Golden Ratio as divine beauty. (1497)
- Psalm 19:1–4, Holy Bible (NIV). "The heavens declare the glory of God…" Quoted as divine geometry in creation.
- Kepler, Johannes. Harmonices Mundi. Argued that planets moved in divine mathematical harmony. (1619)
- Job 38:5, Holy Bible (NIV). "Who marked off its dimensions? Surely you know!" Spoken by God to Job about creation's measurement.
- Isaac Newton, Principia Mathematica. On divine order expressed in physical laws—used to bridge math and spirit. (1687)
- Nature article: "DNA's Double Helix and the Golden Ratio" Cites the approximate appearance of Phi (1.618) in biological spirals. (2010)
- Ephesians 3:18, Holy Bible (NIV). "How wide and long and high and deep is the love of Christ…" Four dimensions of divine math.
- Leonardo da Vinci, anatomical notebooks. Used precise ratios to draw human limbs, teeth, and bones—visibly aligned to Golden Ratio.

- Romans 1:20, Holy Bible (NIV). "For since the creation of the world God's invisible qualities... have been clearly seen..." Foundational verse for math as theology.

Chapter VI: The Eyes, the Ears, the Jaw—What the Organs Preach

- Leonardo da Vinci, Anatomical Studies of the Head and Neck. His detailed sketches of the eye muscles, inner ear canals, and jaw bone reveal his belief that form reveals truth. (c. 1508–1510)
- Proverbs 20:12, Holy Bible (NIV). "Ears that hear and eyes that see—the Lord has made them both."
- Psalm 94:9, Holy Bible (NIV). "Does He who fashioned the ear not hear? Does He who formed the eye not see?" Establishing divine intention in organ creation.
- Matthew 6:22, Holy Bible (NIV). "The eye is the lamp of the body..." Foundational to interpreting the eye as a spiritual gateway.
- Galen of Pergamon, On the Usefulness of the Parts of the Body. Ancient anatomical treatise describing the jaw and ear in detailed physiological terms. (2nd century CE)
- James 1:19, Holy Bible (NIV). "Everyone should be quick to listen, slow to speak..." Used to discuss ear and jaw balance.
- Ezekiel 3:2–3, Holy Bible (NIV). Ezekiel eats the scroll—symbolic of the jaw's prophetic use, not just physical speech.
- Medical article: "The Cochlea and Sound Frequency Interpretation"
- Scientific support for the spiral structure of the inner ear as mathematically tuned. (Journal of Auditory Neuroscience, 2014)
- Isaiah 50:4–5, Holy Bible (NIV). "He wakens me morning by morning, wakens my ear to listen like one being instructed..."
- Psalm 81:10, Holy Bible (NIV). "Open wide your mouth and I will fill it..." Interpreted both physically and spiritually in context of the jaw as altar.

Chapter VII: The Heart and the Sacred Rhythm

- Leonardo da Vinci, Studies of the Heart and Aorta. Considered the most accurate drawings of the heart until modern imaging—Leonardo sketched the aortic valve in motion. (c. 1513)
- Proverbs 4:23, Holy Bible (NIV). "Above all else, guard your heart, for everything you do flows from it."

- 1 Samuel 16:7, Holy Bible (NIV). "Man looks at the outward appearance, but the Lord looks at the heart."
- Ecclesiastes 3:11, Holy Bible (NIV). "He has set eternity in the human heart…" Supporting the heart as divine memory.
- St. Augustine, Confessions, Book I. "You have made us for Yourself, O Lord, and our heart is restless until it rests in You."
- Medical article: "The Heart's Electromagnetic Field and Human Emotion" From HeartMate Institute; confirms the heart's measurable biofield. (2012)
- 2 Corinthians 3:3, Holy Bible (NIV). "You are a letter from Christ… written not with ink but with the Spirit of the living God, not on tablets of stone but on tablets of human hearts."
- Psalm 51:10, Holy Bible (NIV). "Create in me a pure heart, O God, and renew a steadfast spirit within me." Da Vinci, quote from his journals "The heart is a muscle that serves the soul." (Translated, Richter edition)
- John 7:38, Holy Bible (NIV). "Whoever believes in me… rivers of living water will flow from within them." Used to reflect heartbeat as sacred river.

Chapter VII: Breath, Bone, and Body as Scroll

- Ezekiel 37:1–10, Holy Bible (NIV). The Valley of Dry Bones passage, central to the chapter's theme of resurrection, bone, and breath.
- Genesis 2:7, Holy Bible (NIV). "The Lord God… breathed into his nostrils the breath of life." Used as foundational divine design verse.
- Leonardo da Vinci, Musculature of the Spine and Ribs. His layered drawings of the rib cage show a fascination with symmetry and spiritual metaphor. (c. 1509)
- Hebrews 4:12, Holy Bible (NIV). "Sharper than any double-edged sword… it divides soul and spirit, joints and marrow."
- Book of Isaiah 42:5, Holy Bible (NIV). "He who gives breath to its people, and life to those who walk on it…"
- Job 33:4, Holy Bible (NIV). "The Spirit of God has made me; the breath of the Almighty gives me life."
- Medical article: "Osteocytes as Communicators of Mechanical and Spiritual Stress" Suggests bones transmit more than physical data—used metaphorically. (Bone Journal, 2017)
- John 20:22, Holy Bible (NIV). "And with that he breathed on them and said, 'Receive the Holy Spirit.'"

- Revelation 10:9–10, Holy Bible (NIV). John eats the scroll—mirrored metaphor of body as scroll to be digested and declared.
- Psalm 102:18, Holy Bible (NIV). "Let this be written for a future generation…" Interpreted in context of bones as prophecy written in flesh.

Chapter IX: The Temple of Man

- 1 Corinthians 6:19–20, Holy Bible (NIV). "Do you not know that your bodies are temples of the Holy Spirit…?" Central theme of this chapter.
- Exodus 25:9, Holy Bible (NIV). "Make this tabernacle… exactly like the pattern I will show you." Establishes divine blueprint for sacred structure.
- Ezekiel 40–43, Holy Bible (NIV). Ezekiel's vision of the temple measured with exact precision—mirrored in the human body. Leonardo da Vinci, Vitruvian Man (Codex Atlanticus).
- The square/circle combination reflects the cube of Solomon's Holy of Holies (1 Kings 6:20).
- 1 Kings 6:20, Holy Bible (NIV). "The inner sanctuary was twenty cubits long, twenty wide and twenty high." A perfect cube—echoed in human proportion.
- Josephus, The Antiquities of the Jews, Book VIII. Describes the temple layout and materials; used to link with bodily composition. (c. 93–94 AD)
- Hebrews 9:24, Holy Bible (NIV). "Christ did not enter a sanctuary made with human hands…" Spiritual transition from temple to body.
- Psalm 144:12, Holy Bible (NIV). "Our sons in their youth will be like well-nurtured plants, and our daughters will be like pillars carved to adorn a palace." Imagery connecting youth and temple form.
- Michelangelo's Pietà, St. Peter's Basilica. Sculpture places human suffering inside architectural stillness—used symbolically.
- Revelation 21:22, Holy Bible (NIV). "I did not see a temple in the city, because the Lord God Almighty and the Lamb are its temple."

Chapter X: The Final Unveiling—Man as Messenger

- 2 Corinthians 3:2–3, Holy Bible (NIV). "You are a letter from Christ… written not with ink but with the Spirit of the living God…"
- Isaiah 52:7, Holy Bible (NIV). "How beautiful… are the feet of those who bring good news…"
- Leonardo da Vinci, Last Supper, Milan. Compositionally read as a scroll—the apostles arranged like letters around Christ, the Word.
- Romans 10:14–15, Holy Bible (NIV). "How can they hear without someone preaching to them?" Reference to the calling embedded in the body.
- Revelation 10:9–10, Holy Bible (NIV). John eats the scroll—parallel to human beings becoming the message.
- Isaiah 49:2, Holy Bible (NIV). "He made my mouth like a sharpened sword, in the shadow of his hand he hid me."
- Michelangelo's David. Artistic example of human form used to send political and spiritual messages—interpreted in this chapter. Plato, Phaedrus. The soul as a divine chariot—used metaphorically to explore the body as vehicle of message.
- Hebrews 1:1–3, Holy Bible (NIV). "In these last days he has spoken to us by his Son…" Christ as both message and messenger.
- John 1:14, Holy Bible (NIV). "The Word became flesh and made his dwelling among us." The theological climax—man becomes the embodied Word.

Chapter X1: Heaven's Proportions in Woman

- Genesis 2:21–23, Holy Bible (NIV). The creation of woman from man's side—not from the head or foot, but from the heart's rib.
- Song of Songs 4:7, Holy Bible (NIV). "You are altogether beautiful, my darling; there is no flaw in you." Root verse for divine proportion in feminine form.
- Leonardo da Vinci, Female Head Studies, Windsor Collection. Leonardo's rarely known studies of female proportion —delicate geometry, softer ratios. (c. 1508)
- Proverbs 31:25–26, Holy Bible (NIV). "She is clothed with strength and dignity… speaks with wisdom, and faithful instruction is on her tongue."
- Psalm 45:13–14, Holy Bible (NIV). "All glorious is the princess within her chamber; her gown is interwoven with gold."

- Luke 1:28, Holy Bible (NIV). "Greetings, you who are highly favored! The Lord is with you." Angelic address to Mary—beginning of divine incarnation through woman.
- Michelangelo's Libyan Sibyl, Sistine Chapel. Shows a powerful, muscular woman—challenging Renaissance norms and elevating feminine strength.
- Isaiah 66:13, Holy Bible (NIV). "As a mother comforts her child, so will I comfort you..." The maternal form as a reflection of divine compassion.
- Da Vinci's quote on symmetry "Beauty is symmetry governed by the soul." (from Codex Urbinas)
- Galatians 4:4, Holy Bible (NIV). "God sent his Son, born of a woman..." The final alignment: divine destiny proportioned through the feminine body.

Chapter XII: The Geometry of Resurrection—From Dust to Glory

- Ezekiel 37:1–14, Holy Bible, NIV. This passage forms the prophetic foundation for the resurrection of bones, the reassembly of structure, and the divine breath bringing life.
- 1 Corinthians 15:42–44, Holy Bible, NIV. Paul's description of the body as a seed echoes the transformation from perishable to imperishable and supports the metaphor of resurrection geometry.
- Psalm 139:15–16, Holy Bible, NIV. Referenced to underscore God's intimate knowledge of the body's frame, "woven together in the depths of the earth."
- Leonardo da Vinci, Codex Windsor, c. 1510. Anatomical drawings exploring the skeletal system and proportions of bone—used here to reflect divine architecture.
- Leonardo da Vinci, Codex Atlanticus, folios 187r, 237v. Leonardo speculated about the function and symbolism of bones, suggesting a theological and structural interest beyond pure anatomy.
- Vitruvius, De Architectura, Book III. Vitruvian ideas of symmetry and measurement, particularly when applied to the skeleton, lay the groundwork for interpreting the body as a proportional system of resurrection.
- Talmud Bavli, Berakhot 58b. Discusses the "Luz bone," the indestructible bone from which resurrection will one day occur—a concept echoed in the chapter's theology.

- Zohar (Book of Radiance), Vol. I, Folio 218b. Mystical Jewish text referencing divine blueprints embedded in the body, relevant to the theme of sacred architecture and resurrection.
- Plato, Phaedo, Sections 70–72. Plato's theory of the soul's immortality and the body as a temporary vessel frames the contrast between dust and eternal form.
- Michelangelo, The Last Judgment, Sistine Chapel, 1536–1541. Visual inspiration for bodies rising in spiraled motion, with divine breath reordering form and geometry.
- C.S. Lewis, Miracles, Chapter 16: "The Grand Miracle." Lewis reflects on Christ's resurrection as a prototype of all transformation, directly informing the theological lens of this chapter.
- Anatomical Study of the Human Skeleton, Gray's Anatomy, 41st Edition. Used for detailed structure and memory storage of bones, including calcium's role in long-term biological signaling.
- Fibonacci Sequence, in relation to osteology and natural patterning, referenced through applied geometric ratios in biological structure.
- Ecclesiastes 12:7, Holy Bible, KJV. "Then shall the dust return to the earth as it was: and the spirit shall return unto God who gave it"— referenced to unify the biblical arc of dust to glory.
- Romans 8:11, Holy Bible, NIV. "He who raised Christ… will also give life to your mortal bodies…"—directly reinforcing divine reassembly and structural resurrection.
- Leonardo da Vinci, Vitruvian Man, c. 1490, Gallerie dell'Accademia, Venice. The foundational image for this entire study; in this chapter, the drawing is no longer treated as static art, but as an oracular scroll. Every insight culminates here.
- Genesis 2:7, Holy Bible, NIV. "Then the Lord God formed man from the dust… and breathed into his nostrils the breath of life"— used to define both the origin and divine animation of the figure.
- Job 33:4, Holy Bible, NIV. "The Spirit of God has made me; the breath of the Almighty gives me life"—echoing the idea that the drawing breathes when it is understood spiritually.
- Plato, Timaeus, 30B–31A. The universe and man are built on the same divine ratio; this undergirds the argument that the Vitruvian Man is a microcosm of divine geometry.
- Leonardo da Vinci, Codex Leicester, c. 1506– 1510. Notes on the flow of water and movement of spirit as metaphors for understanding invisible forces in nature and man—referenced in describing the hidden voice of the drawing.

- Romans 1:20, Holy Bible, NIV. "For since the creation of the world God's invisible qualities... have been clearly seen..."—supports the thesis that God's truth is etched visibly into the body.
- The Gospel of John 1:14, Holy Bible, NIV. "And the Word became flesh..."—used in reference to the idea that the drawing speaks, just as the Logos was made incarnate.
- Michelangelo Buonarroti, Creation of Adam, Sistine Chapel, 1512. The almost-touching hands parallel the tension between potential and manifestation—the same breath- hovering energy said to animate the Vitruvian figure in the Epilogue.
- The Zohar, Vol. II, Folio 94b. Describes how the letters of the Torah are inscribed in the body; the image of man as "divine parchment" is echoed in this final chapter.
- C.S. Lewis, The Weight of Glory, Essay 1. "You have never talked to a mere mortal..."—quoted to emphasize the eternal and sacred voice encoded in human form.
- Ezekiel 1:10; 10:14, Holy Bible, NIV. Four faces of the cherubim as symbolic geometry— used to reflect layered meaning in man's structure, voice, and spiritual function.
- Isaiah 49:16, Holy Bible, NIV. "See, I have engraved you on the palms of My hands"—used to validate the metaphor of man as a divine drawing.
- Revelation 5:1–5, Holy Bible, NIV. The sealed scroll imagery ties into the idea that Leonardo's drawing is a scroll only the Lamb can truly open—a divine text in visual form.
- Hannah Arendt, The Human Condition, Part II: Labor, Work, Action. Referenced to distinguish between man as product of nature, artifact of creation, and being of purpose—used to interpret the final activation of the drawing.
- Damiano B. Centola, The Mystery of Mysteries: Unveiling the Divine Code of the Vitruvian Man, Chapter 1–12. The Epilogue draws directly from insights, diagrams, and theological arguments established in previous chapters, culminating in a holistic reading of man as message.

Chapter XIII Epilogue: When the Drawing Speaks; The Line, the Breath, and the Flame

- John 1:1, Holy Bible (NIV). "In the beginning was the Word, and the Word was with God, and the Word was God." This establishes that logos (Word) is both blueprint and Being.
- Habakkuk 2:2, Holy Bible (NIV). "Write down the revelation and make it plain on tablets…" This inspired the metaphor of the body as scroll and divine message.
- Isaiah 44:24, Holy Bible (NIV). "I am the Lord, the Maker of all things, who stretches out the heavens…" Used to frame God as both artist and architect.
- Revelation 21:5, Holy Bible (NIV). "Behold, I am making all things new!"—the divine announcement of completed re-creation, as seen in the final understanding of the body.
- Leonardo da Vinci, Codex Arundel, Note 67v. "The body is not a thing—it is a question." This philosophical fragment was a driving idea behind the epilogue.
- Romans 8:19, Holy Bible (NIV). "For the creation waits in eager expectation for the children of God to be revealed." The Vitruvian Man, now fully seen, is part of that unveiling.
- 2 Corinthians 4:7, Holy Bible (NIV). "We have this treasure in jars of clay…" The human body as sacred vessel—imperfect but chosen.
- Ecclesiastes 3:11, Holy Bible (NIV). "He has made everything beautiful in its time. He has also set eternity in the human heart…"
- Psalm 8:4–6, Holy Bible (NIV). "What is mankind that you are mindful of them… You made them a little lower than the angels and crowned them with glory and honor."
- Isaiah 43:21, Holy Bible (NIV). "The people I formed for myself that they may proclaim my praise." The final declaration: that man is not only drawn, but destined to sing.

Final Bibliography & References

Scripture (Holy Bible)

All verses cited from the Holy Bible, New International Version (NIV) unless otherwise noted.

Additional translations used sparingly: King James Version (KJV).

- Genesis 1:26–27; 2:7, 21–23
- Exodus 25:9; 26:15–25
- Leviticus 26:11–12
- 1 Kings 6:15–20
- Psalm 8:4–6; 18:19; 19:1–4; 42:5; 45:13–14;
- 51:10; 81:10; 94:9; 102:18; 139:13–16; 144:12
- Proverbs 4:23; 20:12; 31:25–26
- Ecclesiastes 3:1–11
- Isaiah 40:12; 42:5; 43:21; 44:24; 49:2, 16; 50:4–5;
- 52:7; 53:2; 66:13
- Ezekiel 3:2–3; 16:4–6; 37:1–10; 40–43
- Daniel 7:9–10
- Habakkuk 2:2
- Matthew 6:22
- Luke 1:28
- John 1:1, 14; 7:38; 20:22
- Romans 1:20; 7:15–25; 8:19; 10:14–15
- 1 Corinthians 6:19–20
- 2 Corinthians 3:2–3; 4:7
- Galatians 4:4
- Ephesians 3:18
- Hebrews 1:1–3; 4:12; 9:24
- Revelation 10:9–10; 21:5, 22

Historical and Philosophical Works

- Vitruvius, Marcus Pollio — De Architectura, Book III
- Plato — Republic, Phaedrus, Timaeus
- Aristotle — On the Soul
- St. Augustine — Confessions, Book I
- Josephus — Antiquities of the Jews, Book VIII
- The Zohar (Bereshit A) — Classical Jewish mysticism
- Pythagoras — Fragmentary teachings on number and Harmony
- Kepler, Johannes — Harmonices Mundi (1619)
- Newton, Isaac — Philosophiæ Naturalis Principia Mathematica (1687)
- Greenblatt, Stephen — The Swerve: How the World Became Modern (2011)
- Arendt, Hannah — The Human Condition (1958)
- Vasari, Giorgio — Lives of the Artists (1550)

Leonardo da Vinci – Primary Sources

- Codex Atlanticus — folio 218r (Vitruvian Man)
- Codex Windsor — fetal development & head anatomy
- Codex Arundel — reflections on body as question
- Notebooks, trans. Jean Paul Richter— quotes and proportional theories
- Illustrations for Luca Pacioli — De Divina Proportione (1497)
- Drawings of female head, muscles, ribs, heart, aorta, spine

Scientific and Medical Sources

- Journal of Auditory Neuroscience — "The Cochlea and Sound Frequency Interpretation" (2014)
- Bone Journal — "Osteocytes and Mechanical/ Spiritual Stress" (2017)
- HeartMath Institute — "The Heart's Electromagnetic Field and Human Emotion" (2012)
- Nature— "DNA's Double Helix and the Golden Ratio" (2010)

Artworks Referenced

- Leonardo da Vinci — Vitruvian Man, The Last Supper
- Michelangelo — David, Pietà, Libyan Sibyl, Slaves
- Sistine Chapel — ceiling frescoes
- Creation of Adam — detail: God's finger to Adam's navel

Appendix: Further Meditations, Patterns, and Proofs

This appendix includes material for those who wish to explore The Mystery of Mysteries beyond the written word—into math, theology, anatomy, and divine imagination. It's a space where intellect and awe coexist.

I.   The Golden Ratio in the Human Body

Body Part Pair	Approximate Ratio (cm)	Golden Ratio Presence
Navel to floor/Height	~0.618	✓
Shoulder to fingers/Head to fingers	~0.618	✓
Knee to floor/Hip to floor	~0.618	✓
Arm/Forearm	~0.618	✓

"From the crown of your head to the sole of your feet, your frame preaches symmetry.Organ Shapes and Symbolic Meaning

II.   Organ Shapes and Symbolic Meaning

Organ	Shape	Spiritual Symbolism
Heart	Conic Spiral	Divine rhythm, love
Eye	Spherical Lens	Perception, spiritual sight
Ear	Spiral Cochlea	Revelation, hearing of God
Lung	Branching Tree	Breath of life, Holy Spirit
Jaw	Anchor Arc	Speech, authority, altar of word
Rib	Protective Arc	Covenant, relationship, creation of woman

III.   Fibonacci Numbers in Creation
1, 1, 2, 3, 5, 8, 13, 21, 34, 55, 89, 144...

- Petals on flowers (e.g., lilies, daisies)
- Spiral arms of galaxies
- Pinecones, shells, storms
- Human hand bones (phalange patterns)

IV.   Recommended Areas for Further Study

- Proportional Theology
- Sacred Geometry
- Bioenergetics and the Electromagnetic Body
- Hebrew Alphabet & DNA parallels
- Architecture of the Tabernacle & Human Anatomy"
- Quantum Theology: Body as light/form frequency

V. Key Terms and Glossary

Term	Definition
Vitruvian	Relating to Vituvius, Roman architect whose proportions inspired Da Vinci.
Phi (Φ)	1.618…Golden Ratio, a divine mathematical constant.
Symmetry	Harmony of parts to the whole
Scroll	In biblical context, a written revelation or living message.
Temple	Dwelling place of the divine— now seen as a human body.
Duality	The tension and unity of opposites: motion/rest, matter/spirit.

Note on Proportions and Diagrams

The proportions and diagrams presented in this book are intended to illustrate symbolic, theological, and historical insights drawn from Scripture, art, and sacred geometry. While grounded in anatomical and mathematical research, they represent interpretive models rather than clinical or universally precise measurements of the human body. Their purpose is not to claim absolute scientific accuracy but to reveal the patterns by which artists, architects, and theologians have discerned divine order in creation.

Acknowledgments

This book was not written alone.

I thank God, the Divine Author, for the breath, the design, and the voice behind every syllable herein.

To Leonardo da Vinci—thank you for sketching what others feared to question. You drew man in motion and froze eternity in a frame. You were not just a scientist or artist. You were a seer.

To my wife, Feebe—your music, patience, and fire echo through every page. This work stands because of your faith beside mine.

To every scholar, theologian, scientist, artist, and thinker whose paths I traced and stretched—this book is my offering of unity
across disciplines.

To the readers—poets, builders, skeptics, seekers, mystics—may this book unroll like a scroll, written upon the marrow of your being.

May you see yourself not as flawed, but as frame. Not as chaos, but as code.

And finally—to my own soul, and to the sacred soul of mankind: He who measured the heavens first measured himself.

— Writer Damiano B. Centola

About the Author

Damiano B. Centola is a writer, poet, theologian, and visionary thinker whose work bridges the disciplines of sacred art, anatomy, philosophy, and divine revelation. With a voice rooted in scripture and a mind awakened by geometry, Damiano has become a leading spiritual pioneer in uncovering the mysteries of God's design embedded in the human body.

Born of Sicilian heritage and raised between cultures and continents, Damiano embodies a rare blend of intellectual depth and passionate soul. He writes not simply to inform, but to ignite—to call forth in every reader the eternal code etched into their being by the Creator Himself. Damiano's background spans decades of theological study, literary craftsmanship, and spiritual mentorship. He is the author of numerous works, including:

- God's Sovereignty: Exploring the Divine Rule Over Creation, History, and Eternity
- The Mother of Corruption: Unveiling Spiritual Corruption from Babylon to Today
- Divine Encounters: Discovering the Depth and Power of God's Names
- I Choose the Call: My Daily Anthem of Devotion A Journey of Faith, Purpose, and Obedience
- The Lord Is My Shepherd: A Journey Through Psalm 23

www.ingramcontent.com/pod-product-compliance
Lightning Source LLC
Chambersburg PA
CBHW051205120626
46547CB00013B/1204